Sunshine

BOOKS AUTHORED OR COAUTHORED
BY ELAINE CANNON

Adversity

As a Woman Thinketh

Baptized and Confirmed: Your Lifeline to Heaven

Be a Bell Ringer

Bedtime Stories for Grownups

Beyond Baptism: A Guide for New Converts

Boy of the Land, Man of the Lord

Called to Serve Him

Corner on Youth

Eight Is Great

The Girl's Book

God Bless the Sick and Afflicted

Heart to Heart

Life—One to a Customer

Love You

Merry, Merry Christmases

The Mighty Change

Mothering

Mothers and "Other Mothers"

Not Just Ordinary Young Men and Young Women

Notable Quotables

Putting Life in Your Life Story

Quote Unquote

The Seasoning

The Summer of My Content

The Time of Your Life

Turning Twelve or More: Living by the Articles of Faith

Elaine Cannon

BOOKCRAFT
Salt Lake City, Utah

Copyright © 1994 by Bookcraft, Inc.

All rights reserved. No part of this book may be repro-
duced in any form or by any means without permission
in writing from the publisher, Bookcraft, Inc., 1848 West
2300 South, Salt Lake City, Utah 84119.

Bookcraft is a registered trademark of Bookcraft, Inc.

Library of Congress Catalog Card Number: 94-78749
ISBN 0-88494-955-9

Second Printing, 1995

Printed in the United States of America

There Is Sunshine in My Soul Today

There is sunshine in my soul today,
More glorious and bright
Than glows in any earthly sky,
For Jesus is my light.

There is music in my soul today,
A carol to my King,
And Jesus listening can hear
The songs I cannot sing.

There is springtime in my soul today,
For when the Lord is near,
The dove of peace sings in my heart,
The flow'rs of grace appear.

There is gladness in my soul today,
And hope and praise and love,
For blessings which he gives me now,
For joys "laid up" above.

Oh, there's sunshine, blessed sunshine
When the peaceful happy moments roll.
When Jesus shows his smiling face,
There is sunshine in the soul.

(Eliza E. Hewitt, *Hymns,* no. 227.)

Contents

There Is Sunshine in My Soul Today

"There is sunshine in my soul and gladness in my heart" are the brave words of those hardy, happy souls who see the silver lining in dark clouds and the butterfly in the fat, repulsive caterpillar on the green sprout. Such people belong to the "Men Are, That They Might Have Joy" Club, and they are willing to hold out until forever to reap their reward.

In the Doctrine and Covenants the promise of joy has been defined with a timetable of *not* now and *not* in this world. We are promised a spiritual joy in Christ, and this we should seek avidly. Joseph Smith received this revelation of comfort in Kirtland, Ohio, when the Saints who had gathered in Missouri were suffering excruciating persecutions of all kinds. They were in despair. The Lord comforted Joseph, "Wherefore, fear not even unto death; for in this world your joy is not full, but in me your joy is full" (101:36). The whole plan and purpose of life is to bring about gladness in our hearts and to prepare us for an eternity of joy—ultimately, *ultimately*—when the soul and the body are interminably bonded together and capable of the fulness of joy after the manner of Christ.

Meanwhile, back on earth, we reach for making the most happiness out of what we have to live with.

My two grandmothers were poles apart but I loved each of them dearly. One was generations deep in Church membership and strictness of standards. The other was a convert, an immigrant, whose small pleasures came from the beverages she'd learned to use in the old country. The first wanted me to be good. The second wanted me to be happy because she thought I *was* good. I figured this out as a young girl and marveled at how much depends upon the way life is viewed. As the years passed I realized that being good brings happiness. And the grandmothers weren't so far from each other after all.

Given the parameters of mortality, given the nature of humans, given the path people tread, we must find our pleasurable moments along the way. The guide for doing this is as close as the glad tidings found in the standard works.

The scriptures speak of being "girded with gladness" and "anointed with the oil of gladness." This is highly descriptive. Indeed, why settle for a fleeting spot of happiness when you can be girded with it—swathed in it, wrapped about with it, bathed and anointed with such gladness? The imagery is akin to all the shining, smooth countenances you have ever seen, the clearest, most placid mountain lakes you've watched at sunset, the brightness and lightness and sparkle that have enhanced your memories.

But for all that, standing in front of a mirror and telling yourself, "I'm feeling glad; I'm so glad I'm feeling glad!" doesn't necessarily make it so. Even when we ought to be happy we may instead feel jealous, angry, impatient, disappointed. Perhaps we will need to follow the pattern of Enos and Alma and even Jacob and wrestle before God for a remission of simple sins or great ones before such peace and happiness can be ours. Joy and gladness come when we have earned them, when we are prepared to receive them.

What qualities make for gladness? Peace; forgiveness, both given and received; confidence before God; virtue garnishing thoughts; principles applied; beauty in unexpected places and times, like the forgotten bulb that becomes a tulip in a compost pile—the unlooked-for blossom is a living symbol that good can spring from a dung heap.

Sometimes the innate strength and hope of the human soul surface only in times of catastrophe or unduly trying circumstance. This is so in the account of the Jaredites. They had undertaken the long and arduous journey of being blown across the sea—three hundred and forty-four days upon the water. It must have been a most difficult trip. When at last they had landed upon the shore of the promised land and had put foot on solid ground, these valiant people "bowed themselves down upon the face of the land, and did humble themselves before the Lord, and did shed tears of joy before the Lord, because of the multitude of his tender mercies over them" (Ether 6:12).

The Jaredites are a prototype. May you be *that* glad with your own lot.

The bottom line in this life is that the closer you come to Christ and to his creations, the happier you will be. Look for the blessings and enjoy them! Then will there be sunshine in your soul no matter what lumps show up in life. In *Sunshine* you will find success stories and descriptions of situations that can rekindle your spirit and spark your heart into gladness. And you will read about the possibilities in life that can generate happiness no matter what else is going on!

1

There Is Gladness in My Soul Today

Gladness is not equated with ownership, with belongings. There must be more to life than having everything. There must be an acquisition beyond the acquisition of things. There has to be value, happiness, and peace available to all God's children regardless of their financial standing.

The peaceable things and gladness come from God for the asking. The exact wording of the telling scripture is: "If thou shalt ask, thou shalt receive revelation upon revelation, knowledge upon knowledge, that thou mayest know the mysteries and peaceable things—that which bringeth joy, that which bringeth life eternal" (D&C 42:61).

Counting one's blessings is one of the peaceable things. This inevitably brings forth gladness and generates such sunshine in the soul that dark clouds are dispelled. It is the matter of focusing either on the little bucket going down into the well empty or on the little bucket coming up full. Attitude. Perspective.

Louise Lake once described counting blessings as an "exercise in joy." For many years I have used that phrase widely. Surely it surfaced in my heart again as I worked on this book. Louise was a tragically stricken invalid who for thirty-five years invariably counted each day a bonus that was filled with things to be grateful for. This dear woman, friend to many, is deceased now. However, in this setting I give her a salute of thanks for being an example of gallant gladness when life turned up terrible as well as when things were going well. Over and over again she would say how glad she was that she could count on God to get her through whatever.

My own mother was a powerful, experienced, joyful teacher of the gospel. She lived all of her life as a true believer in application of principles and in service, but on her deathbed I was startled—surprisingly to me—by a new dimension of her belief. She was so very still as I sat by her bed. I thought she might have already passed on. "Mother. Mother!" I gently insisted upon a response by pressing more firmly on the hand I held. Yes, she was old now (and I was getting there too) and she deserved to die, but letting go of someone I still needed so much was more painful than I had reckoned. "Mother, are you all right?"

And then she spoke softly, "I'm all right." Her eyelids opened a bit, releasing a spill of tears down her cheeks. She kept moving her dear head slowly from side to side in a familiar bit of body language that signified wonder, marvel, ecstasy. "The dear Lord is helping me!" These were her last words to me.

Her belief brought her joy. Mine now brings me gladness through gratitude. Surely you have found this true, as well— that an awareness of one's blessings and the giver of them inevitably brings wonder, gladness, joy. C. S. Lewis said joy should be distinguished from pleasure and happiness. About joy he simply said that "anyone who has experienced it will want it again." (*Surprised by Joy* [New York: Harcourt Brace and Co., 1956], p. 18.)

A new dimension comes to all of life when life is viewed with a "gospel heart." Alma writes these amazing, thought-provoking lines that send the soul on a search for its own glorious gladness: "And this is the account of Ammon and his brethren, their journeyings in the land of Nephi, their sufferings in the land, their sorrows, and their afflictions, and their *incomprehensible joy*. . . . And now may the Lord, the

Redeemer of all men, bless their souls forever." (Alma 28:8, emphasis added.)

And yours!

Thornton Wilder is praised yet for his 1938 play *Our Town* in which the audience is lifted high to their own precious memories—an awareness of blessings uncounted before, perhaps. Remember Emily's return to life for one day? After viewing her family, she weeps and cries out: "It goes so fast. We don't have time to look at one another. I didn't realize. So all that was going on and we never noticed. . . . One more look. Good-by, Good-by, world. . . . Good-by to clocks ticking . . . and Mama's sunflowers. . . . And new-ironed dresses and hot baths . . . and sleeping and waking up." (*Our Town* [New York: Harper Perennial, 1992], p. 100.) At last, having *realized* her wonderful world, and drunk it in, Emily was ready to go on to heaven.

People who have been through a brush with death or failure, or who have come close to being entrapped by sin but then have been saved—such people often view life with wider eyes and a warmer heart. Each day is a gift.

I remember weeks of thick fog. There was a certain beauty in the frost-flocked trees, their naked structures clothed now, protected against the low temperatures winter weather brought. But mostly there was the enveloping, smothering, depressing fog. Then long weeks after, the sun broke through. Oh, the rejoicing!

Life is like this—life understood by studying nature. This and watching one's mother be "helped to die" by the Lord have some link with working for several years on a book and at last putting it to press. It is to be overcome with the gladness of gratitude at all connected with its preparation: Heavenly Father so gracious in response to persistent pleadings and grave expressions of appreciation, and so generous with inspiration; people who help, people who were object lessons and examples; the wisdom of the ages that is brought to mind. It is true that *realizing* everyday associations, moments of sudden understanding, and closeness to the Lord under whatever circumstances unfolds myriad blessings in the heart. Then come gladness and sunshine in the soul.

The Lord said, "And he who receiveth all things with thankfulness shall be made glorious; and the things of this earth shall be added unto him, even an hundred fold, yea, more" (D&C 78:19). Count your many blessings!

To get the reader into the mood of this book I asked Mabel Jones Gabbott to compose poetry about the promise of gladness. Mabel and I shared happy days on the staff of the *Improvement Era*. Some of her poems have been set to music and have become favorite hymns of worship. They are especially appropriate in helping to set the necessary spiritual mood for the sacrament. Mabel is a woman of warm awareness of the Lord's goodness to us all. I am grateful to Mabel for her talent and her effort.

To Walk in Gladness

"I came to bring you life," He said.
Life more abundant, more beautiful;
He moved among us with word and deed,
Leaving a pattern rich and full.

He opened windows in closed minds;
He stirred the quiet pulse to give.
He wakened goodness in the hearts
And challenged us to be, *to live!*

Oh, let us shape our days like His
And in His name serve those in need.
Let's make the world a sweeter place
By giving self in loving deed.

For all He asks is simply this:
That we choose God all life long
And love each other, as He taught,
And walk in gladness and in song.

—Mabel Jones Gabbott

The Psalms have something for every situation, it seems. They even include a recipe for joy and gladness: "Thou lovest righteousness, and hatest wickedness: therefore God, thy God, hath anointed thee with the oil of gladness above thy fellows" (Psalm 45:7).

Precious, helpful truths are learned through the gospel of Jesus Christ. In the Church of Jesus Christ, where the gospel is protected and promoted, we find truth, wisdom—as well as knowledge undreamed of—security, peace, hope, and choice opportunities for personal growth. There is purpose in the inimitable, God-given plan. The gospel teaches us about prayer—God does hear and answer our prayers. He knows us by name and heartache. He promises to heal, comfort, and protect us. He will forgive us. He will love us anyway! The Lord is willing, if we are, to guide us safely back to our Heavenly Father. Because of him, no matter what comes in the seasons of life, there will be honey from the rock, love even in loneliness, and inner peace in the presence of terror at midnight. There will be abundance even in the midst of flood, fire, and quake.

Gladness comes in a personal witness that Jesus lives and operates in the affairs of our world. If we will but seek the Lord we will find him, for he is "not far from every one of us: for in him we live, and move, and have our being. . . , For we are also his offspring" (Acts 17:27–28). This I believe. It is the belief that brings me peace and gladness.

The Sabbath day brings gladness in the miracle of renewal of covenants, the sweet solace in hymns, the heightened compassion through being about our Father's business—visiting the sick, the widows, the rejected, and the careworn caregivers, and gathering our families into a semblance of Sunday behavior.

Oh, the gladness in families at any stage and in any mix, with endless mothers and fathers through the generations before and after to be remembered and honored and marveled at!

There is unspeakable joy and gladness in all of this, plus in music, miracles, feasts and traditions, relationships, and fascinating people who are heroes and saints or nicely obscure in their good deeds. Here we find proof that living the gospel, experimenting upon the word, works.

I thank all of you who shared your experiences and perspectives, adding to the wealth of this book. I am forever grateful and warm with love for the inspiring, select few who have been by my side in my long life, whether in friendship, service, or familial links.

Also, there are the beloved ghosts who populate my heart in the night hours. These pleasant recollections stir up such gladness that I almost relish sleeplessness. And I thank God again and again for the countless good things from his hand. "Thou hast turned for me my mourning into dancing: thou hast put off my sackcloth, and girded me with gladness" (Psalm 30:11).

I am akin to Albert Camus, who wrote, "In the midst of winter I find there is in me an invincible summer." Sunshine everywhere, no matter what else is going on.

This book is filled with glad tidings that can be heaped up within your heart like a carpet of rose petals dropped at the season's end. And with all my petals counted, there is gladness in my soul today.

2

There Is Music in My Soul Today

Recently I received a birthday present—a portable CD player for my automobile. It was supposed to make me glad and free from stress. It was from my ever-watchful family. I protested about the gift, not because I lacked appreciation. I protested because I wasn't sure I could handle driving and listening to the sound track from *Schindler's List,* featuring Itzhak Perlman, at the same time. It is so soul shaking! I have trouble enough concentrating on traffic patterns, leftover winter road ruts, and the strange antics of any town's erratic drivers—a nursing mother at the wheel of a van with eight kids aboard; the Big Deal with his cellular phone tucked under his chin and the *Wall Street Journal* spread flat open on the dashboard for easy reference; two timeworn codgers on their way home to Retirement Row from their daily golf go around arguing over every hole; the sweet young thing in her low, lean red convertible weaving through traffic and flying down the passing lane. One thanks God for whatever ministering angels ride the hood of the sports car or the super-truck that is on automatic pilot while the driver gyrates to the beat of belching electronics.

My protests and arguments notwithstanding, the birthday

gift stuck. My family insisted that my life would improve if it were programmed to the counsel of the Psalmist: "Make a joyful noise unto the Lord" (Psalm 98:4).

It would be better all around if I were soothed by magnificent music while I drove from Here to There. It said so, right on the portable CD player's box: "Enjoy superb digital stereo On-the-Go!" Okay! Okay! But first I had to get the portable compact disc digital audio player hooked up. To support the gift, I had to invest in a portable CD player-mount-die-cast-anodized-aluminum-swivel-suspension-system to help prevent the skipping and mistracking that the next rut in the road might produce.

Then I had to purchase a high-current DC power adapter with four coaxial plugs to hook into the dormant cigarette lighter on the dashboard.

Then there was the needful item called a compact disc cassette adapter, which required no permanent installation, just finding out whether your cassette player had a left- or right-side load or a slot in the front.

Then, to power the CD player, the adapter cord had to be inserted in the special cassette, which was inserted into the car's player slot.

Then there was the matter of finding the suitable-to-my-mood compact disc itself to insert in the mounted player, which was plugged into the cigarette lighter on one end and inserted on the other end in the adapter cassette in the car player.

Then I had to turn on the car's sound system and adjust the volume level, and finally I was all set to hear the music. Whoa! If you thought a talking car buzzing you to fasten your seat belt was a tough adjustment, wait until you muscle a portable CD connection! Caution: Better do it before starting up your motor and entering the traffic pattern, or no music under heaven will soothe your nerves.

Then I was told I should lay in a supply of grocery bags under the driver's seat, in which to hide this expensive equipment—once I have disassembled it all upon parking the car in a public place. This is to ward off thieves. It seems that portable CD players are a hot "take-out" item now.

I decided that today's music buffs are a strange lot, with questionable values. All of that fuss and expense over a portable CD player, when switching on the radio is free! But then I played soprano Leontyne Price's classic 1973 recording of *Vier letzte Lieder* (four last songs) by Richard Strauss (CD Papillon Collection, RCA Victor). The sound enveloping me in my own car shifted me to heaven—with my wheels steady on earth. Oh, here is pure, sheer gorgeous music that breeds noble ecstasy with the flip of the on-switch of my new equipment. I thank God for the inspiration provided to composer and vocalist and for the technical genius of digital equipment. What a great birthday gift!

Music is a personal thing, because our emotions are linked to tone, meter, rhythm, key, and arrangement, for example. Music isn't generational. I have a grandson I'm proud of who as a high school senior played guitar with a group while taking classical voice lessons on the side. He's interested in opera. His musical taste is eclectic and mine is selective. I like some opera, most classic jazz, a variety of symphonies, a good male chorus, Diana Ross, and John Williams et al. performing almost anything.

The wind instruments, especially the saxophone or clarinet, are exhilarating. Doc Severinsen and his mellow horn provide good mood music. For a classical soar, listen to Wynton Marsalis in an amazing contrapuntal selection with soprano Edita Gruberová. When I am writing, my taste in music varies with the writing assignment. I'll get buoyed up with a variety of offerings: the Tabernacle Choir singing "Sheep May Safely Graze"; John Rutter's unique religious music, *Gloria;* Nat and Natalie's romantic father-daughter offering, "Unforgettable"; *Wagner Without Words; All Gershwin, Concertos;* Lex de Azevedo's arrangements of Mormon hymns. The hymns evoke a warm feeling of closeness to God without Leontyne's distracting creative swell or Bach's raising the roof, though each has its place.

Hymns, for those of us who have sung them for a span of years, are nostalgic reminders of our various learnings and preparations, as well as the substance of testimony rehearsed again and again, beginning with early childhood song practices featuring the hymns.

Angelyn Hinckley led the singing in our Sunday School when I was young. She was the daughter of an Apostle, Elder Alonzo A. Hinckley, and his saintly wife. So Angelyn was believable. In her own right Angie was an impressive conductor of the hymns because she wore a perpetual smile and used a lot of vigorous arm action. She was no "uncertain trumpet," certainly. She made singing a certain kind of gladness, and we knew that she relished gospel music and gospel truths.

I well remember to this day, umpteen years down the fast lane, a hymn that taught a valuable truth. Angie had us practice over and over and yet again the hymn that contained this startling counsel, "Before you ma-ake a promise, consider well its importance; and when made [long pause] engrave it upon your heart [faster]."

Recently I heard a children's chorus assembled for a special worship service aired on public television. Possibly the sweetest sound on earth is young voices, well trained, singing with rapturous belief. This group was good, and they sang a song from my childhood that I grew up believing. (Whoever sings it anymore? Certainly not the choir directors weaned on diet cola!) I wept through every verse of "In Our Lovely Deseret." This "multitude of children" chorus sang words slightly altered to personalize the song:

> That [we] children may live long
> And be beautiful and strong,
> Tea and coffee and tobacco [we] despise,
> Drink no liquor, and [we] eat
> But a very little meat;
> [We] are seeking to be great and good and wise.
>
> Hark! hark! hark! 'tis children's music—
> Children's voices, oh, how sweet,
> When in innocence and love,
> Like the angels up above,
> They with happy hearts and cheerful faces meet.
>
> (Eliza R. Snow, *Hymns,* no. 307.)

These children sang it straight. President Spencer W. Kimball would have loved it! It reminds me of a regional LDS conference I was assigned to where the special choir sang a "symphonic arrangement" of "Come, Come, Ye Saints." On our way back to the airport President Kimball sadly remarked that while he appreciated the well-meaning efforts, he wished the Saints would remember the gilded-lily lesson in their choral presentations. The inspired version in its simple form was to him the best. His summation of the matter was, "They sang a lot of extra notes, didn't they?"

Just the same, I never heard a more delightful rendering of "We Thank Thee, O God, for a Prophet" than Spencer W. Kimball giving his own "by ear" chorded accompaniment to a duet sung by Harold B. Lee and Ezra Taft Benson—Apostles and prophets and musicians all, as well. Another occasion featured President Lee at the piano for a quartet of fellow Apostles consisting of Matthew Cowley, Ezra Taft Benson, Spencer W. Kimball and Mark E. Petersen.

Longfellow put it this way: "Yes music is the Prophet's art . . . among the gifts that God hath sent . . . one of the most magnificent."

President Kimball was a man of simple tastes. He compared elaborate variations on a favorite and familiar Church hymn to the heavy, laden-with-gold layers of robing and adornment of some religious leaders—such a contrast to the pristine Christ!

Perhaps suitability of music is what's needed. It takes skill to produce variation on a hymn's theme that will be pleasing to a congregation who has sung the hymn repeatedly in its simple, beloved form and is geared to the simple, familiar melody. A classic exception to the preferability of the "unadulterated" hymn arrangement—one which J. Spencer Cornwall, Tabernacle Choir conductor for many years, also espoused—is the magnificent arrangement of "Battle Hymn of the Republic" which ups a familiar religious folk song to a popular, spine-tingling motivator when sung by the choir.

As part of the 1964 New York World's Fair, The Church of Jesus Christ of Latter-day Saints was grudgingly permitted to build its own pavilion. In keeping with Church tradition a lovely dedicatory ceremony was held in that building. The executive leaders of the fair had been invited, and, being curious, they all came! The Church wanted to impress them, of course. Members had come fasting and praying that a good relationship would develop between these professional fair promoters and managers and the Church. So the Spirit was especially rich during the meeting that day.

To fully appreciate what happened next, it is necessary to understand the seating arrangement. The Brethren sat on the stand, while their wives and a few special guests sat close by in the front of the congregation. I was sitting on the second row, right behind Jessie Evans Smith, wife of President Joseph Fielding Smith. The last hymn sung was a resounding salute to what we believe: "The Spirit of God Like a Fire Is Burning." And indeed it was! People dabbed at their eyes. At the last verse Melva Niles and Robert Peterson, gifted musical stars in New York at that time and members of the Manhattan Ward, broke into an obbligato part. As their voices soared above the familiar tune, tears flowed freely and President Smith was sniffling. He did not have a handkerchief, and repeatedly I saw Sister Smith try to pass him her lace-edged, lipstick-stained hankie. He would shake his head each time she reached forward thrusting the feminine linen square. He did not want that solution to his problem. But as the Spirit swelled and his emotions increased, so did his problem. Finally Sister Smith left her seat and crouched forward and thrust her handkerchief into his hand. Just in time! He used it, too.

When I was a little child our whole family went to church—everybody, every time—vacations and holidays notwithstanding. Sometimes sacrament meeting was really interesting, especially when the musical number featured Brother and Sister Clawson, who performed a duet: he played the harmonica and she whistled. They gave a whole new sound to the hymns.

Sometimes young Jessie Evans sang, "He that hath clean hands and a pure heart," in a way that made me look at mine twice—palms up, then palms down. She was blessed with an unusually resonant, deep contralto voice. She had a gift and was well trained, but sometimes her enunciation brought strange expressions to her face, and well, we children had a difficult time not convulsing into loud laughter. She sang often, and we never got used to such a style. To the despair of our mother, we giggled and giggled, stuffing handkerchiefs in our mouths to stifle the sound. We hid our faces in the hymnbooks. Nothing seemed to work until mother tightened her arms in a squeeze about our little shoulders. Such gladness we felt when on occasion she marched us out of the chapel.

Though we spent our growing years imitating Sister Jessie's "c-lean hands and a puuu-re hear-rt [sort of trilling the *r*]," we never forgot the impact of the message. Years later I sat in the congregation of the Solemn Assembly gathered to sustain Joseph Fielding Smith as prophet and President of The Church of Jesus Christ of Latter-day Saints. The Tabernacle Choir featured a longtime, distinguished member, Jessie Evans Smith, wife of the new prophet, as soloist in "He That Hath Clean Hands and a Pure Heart." I wept through the whole wonderful, remarkable presentation. Nobody else seemed so moved as I was on that occasion, and several people later asked questions about it. I admitted that my tears were tears of repentance for my antics in church as a silly child when Jessie Evans was a young woman singing that same song—a song for which she became renowned.

During President Smith's service as a Church leader he and Sister Smith would often sing together in informal settings. The Saints loved this example from such an important couple. On one occasion I was the keynote speaker for a special conference of disabled seminary students. Many were severely handicapped and had speech impediments. I was alerted that President and Sister Smith might put in a surprise visit. If they came in the middle of my speech I was to stop, and while the Smiths walked up the aisle to the stand, the chorister would quickly lead us in a congregational tribute, "We Thank Thee, O God, for a Prophet." That is exactly what happened. It was particularly uplifting to hear the garbled speech and untrained voices of these choice spirits and to watch as they turned their faces toward the Smiths in a singing tribute.

President Smith escorted Sister Jessie up to the stand, where they stopped by the piano. She explained that she and President Smith were going to sing a duet. He then interrupted her and said, "You mean a *do* it, not a duet!" There was laughter from the group, and then the sweet hymn "Love at Home" by the Smiths was followed by greeting and counsel from President Smith to these thrilled young people and their inimitable leaders.

Music has a way of bonding people together. I remember the year when Brigham Young University Travel Studies chartered the beautiful *Mississippi Queen* paddle wheeler, and several hundred LDS people filled the staterooms to float down that great American river. Dallin Oaks, Jeffrey Holland, and I were assigned to give lectures at various historical and cultural sites along the voyage. The experience was enjoyable for us because of the captive audiences we had and the things we learned in preparation. But at that time we agreed that an important part of the experience was the singing that went on between the passengers onboard and the citizens on the bank who crowded the shoreline wherever the boat stopped.

A paddle wheeler is more flexible than an oceangoing ship. On a lovely summer evening we'd pull over against the shore, and we'd lean over the many-leveled railings and call back and forth to the families gathered on grassy banks and weathered docks. It was all spontaneous. We'd sing a song to them and they'd sing a folk tune or Christian hymn to us. Together we'd harmonize on a patriotic song. It was immediate heart-to-heart stuff! And when the paddle wheeler would start up and the whistle would signal our slide back into deep water, there was a show of great tenderness and a kind of sadness as we bid each other good-bye. Somehow we *knew* God's children aren't that different from each other deep down inside.

Skin color of a guest meant problems for the old Hotel Utah. I was society editor of the *Deseret News* at the period when fabulous black singer Marian Anderson was in Salt Lake for a concert at Kingsbury Hall on the University of Utah campus. There was trouble with accommodations for Miss Anderson. No business establishment would risk losing clientele by registering a colored person. It seems unbelievable now, but it was an inflammatory situation then. Remember, the Daughters of the American Revolution had not allowed Miss Anderson to perform in Washington D.C.'s venerable Constitution Hall because of her race! First lady Eleanor

Roosevelt used her clout to protest that decision, and arrangements were made for Miss Anderson to perform a concert on the steps of the Lincoln Memorial.

In Salt Lake for a concert the inimitable Marian Anderson was finally, quietly allowed to be housed at the Hotel Utah, but she was escorted in and out of the building through back doors and the freight elevator. As a newspaperwoman, I was aware of all this before the concert event. My heart ached and I was embarrassed for our city. Perhaps that fact made her appearance all the more poignant and significant to me, though her talent certainly cannot be denied. Here was the singer discriminated against, hiding her hurt in order to perform. When she sang, "Were you there when they crucified my Lord? . . . It caused me to tremble, tremble," *she* trembled. I was near the front and could see her tremble and could note the depth of her empathy, her understanding about the Lord and the all and all of Easter week.

That evening remains a spiritual as well as a musical high. We knew we were in the presence of one of God's noble children. The standing ovation she received proved her popularity, though most of the audience would never know that this great human being had been relegated to the freight elevator and secrecy for her night's lodging after such a performance; we had bonded with her and each other.

This bonding between people when music is part of the scene was evident again at the funeral of Brother Arthur Haycock, who served valiantly as personal secretary to five Presidents of the Church and traveled the world with them. He loved music, flowers, and the dear Polynesian people. In addition, in his lifetime he had served in Hawaii as a young missionary, a mission president, and president of the Hawaii Temple. When the closing prayer had been offered at his funeral, a handsome native Hawaiian stood at the podium unannounced and sang "Aloha Oe" in the Hawaiian language. He invited the congregation to join him in the chorus. With this tender music lovingly sung by all, the lei-draped coffin was taken from the chapel and all the extended family of this good man followed behind. Not until then did the unrehearsed, exquisite a cappella music whisper lovingly to an end.

For a milestone wedding anniversary I asked our children to write their favorite remembrance of their childhood years in our family home. Without exception they all included the special memory of their dad singing them to sleep. At the time he was a busy young bishop with a demanding career that required all-day and late-night work. Yet he'd come home for dinner and stay long enough to sing the children to sleep. This former missionary, who served in Hawaii, positioned himself in the hall servicing their bedrooms, perched on a stool to strum his ukulele, and lulled them with Hawaiian melodies such as "I Loved a Pretty Maui Girl" and folk tunes such as "I've Been Working on the Railroad" and "Abdul da Bulbul Emir."

Music enhances any situation. A small grandson startled me with his accomplished whistle. It was a special delight because always and forever I have been a whistler. We were doing some painting at his home and right away that small boy began to whistle while he worked. How our painting job was lightened by our duets!

Family musical moments are inimitable. Music has a way of sweetening life.

Missionary farewells and homecomings, and funerals too, often feature memorable family musical combinations. A precious bonding inevitably happens. With Mom at the piano, the trio of singing Sharp sisters highlighted a fine brother's homecoming. The sound of the music echoed the gladness in their faces at being all together again after separations by marriages and a mission.

There was a high school boy suffering from a life-threatening illness who requested that his four older sisters gather at his bedside to sing his favorite songs one more time. It was a kind of command performance, and many youthful patients were wheeled in to listen, according to his kind nurse, Rhonda, at Primary Children's Hospital. This young man had been certain that he was dying. The music seemed to sum up his life for him. It reminded him of the little programs at family home evenings as well as the grander occasions like family wedding breakfasts and birthdays, quartet contests in stake Mutual, rehearsals for community back-to-school events. While his sisters sang, the things that mattered most to him suddenly seemed more wonderful than ever. He decided to fight for his life. It worked!

The extended descendants of George Q. Cannon (and that's a crowd!) reveled in the tradition of singing carols of Christmas each year to the remaining members of the first generation—the children (and their spouses) of George Q. Cannon and his five wives. Singing, smiles, and loving embraces said what words never could. The occasion made up for separation because of busy lives. It built a web of familiarity and appreciation among this scattered group of cousins.

There's another kind of love present when friends gather to serenade newlyweds at their celebration. There are songs that make campfire programs, hikes, river trips, long jaunts on the bus some kind of wonderful. I hope some of you dear readers can recall the spirited chant of hikers long ago, "For I am a Boy Trail Builder."

One of the stunning musical moments in any generation is the send-off for missionaries at the Mission Training Center. It is the male chorus harmonizing in the rousing "Ye Elders of Israel."

Another musical memory of note occurred in the Tabernacle on Temple Square during a general women's meeting in the early 1980s when one young woman sang a solo, "You're Not Alone." We had commissioned composer Michael McLean for "something wonderful," and it happened that night. The song has become a hit and is a comfort in many needful situations.

A dramatic occasion stirred a lump in my throat in regard to the faith-promoting hymns and the mellowing power of nostalgic folk songs. Our lovely daughter was in an emergency situation at a university hospital, with medical procedures being administered to her for which no anesthetic could be given. The pain and trauma were extreme. She cried out and writhed in agony. Three doctors and five nurses worked with her, some helping to restrain her. I stood by her head and stroked her hair, mopped her brow, and whispered in her ear. But nothing could soothe this terrible time for her. The suffering conjured up memories of a dreadful experience in her life and added to her stress. She was an adult—a mother herself—but I treated her as my little one again. Quietly I began to sing lullabies into her ear. She responded a bit. Then I sang a hymn and a family favorite. Suddenly she rallied and began to harmonize in her dear, familiar way. She was distracted from the painful procedures under way for which no sedative could be given. She relaxed and turned toward me, lifting a cheek as she sang. It was a holy moment, for as we harmonized in our family song, "Let us all press on in the work of the Lord," the Spirit calmly enveloped us both. We sang for nearly twenty minutes, with the magic of music preparing the soul for the Comforter. She didn't live, but what a grand memory that musical moment was.

Outstanding funeral memories must include the impressive chorus of the posterity of Louise Covey (Mrs. Lynn S.) Richards. A great group stood up from their seats—they occupied many pews past the center mark of the chapel. All ages of Louise's loved ones blended their voices in grief, love, faith, family spirit, and honor for Louise, who was a longtime worker in the Primary program. Appropriately they sang a moving rendition of "I Am a Child of God."

Gifted celebrity performer Robert Peterson once sang "My Cup Runneth O'er with Love" at a gathering of Church leaders. He dedicated the number to President Spencer W. Kimball and his wife, Camilla, who was thrilled with an armful of yellow roses presented by the popular singer—though she admitted that the song was sufficient! At the funeral of the inimitable Keith Engar, former general chairman of the Church activities committee, Brother Peterson melted us all by singing "And This Is My Beloved" from the musical *Kismet*. This was Keith's favorite song, and Brother Peterson dedicated it to Keith's wife, Amy.

These musical moments are heaped up with hundreds more.

Universally, music brings gladness as it opens hearts one to another. Music can do this, not so much because of the particular instruments being played or the tone of a certain human voice, but because of the emotion evoked by the melody, that miraculous series of sounds.

So let the music begin! "Sing aloud unto God our strength: make a joyful noise. . . . Sing unto the Lord a new song," as the Psalms suggest. (81:1; 96:1.) Sing to each other with an emotion that enhances the love we as God's children feel for him and for each other.

After all, what is life for if not to make things more pleasant for each other? How hauntingly this poetry by George Eliot carries out this suggestion:

O May I Join the Choir Invisible

O, may I join the choir invisible
Of those immortal dead who live again
In minds made better by their presence: live
In pulses stirred to generosity,
In deeds of daring rectitude, in scorn
For miserable aims that end with self,
In thoughts sublime that pierce the night like stars,
And with their mild persistence urge man's search
To vaster issues.

. . . .

May I reach
That purest heaven; be to other souls
The cup of strength in some great agony,
Enkindle generous ardor, feed pure love;
Beget the smiles that have no cruelty,
Be the sweet presence of a good diffused,
And in diffusion ever more intense!
So shall I join the choir invisible
Whose music is the gladness of the world.

(In *Masterpieces of Religious Verse,* ed. James
Dalton Morrison [New York: Harper and Row,
1948], pp. 595–96.)

3

When the Peaceful, Happy Moments Roll

In the search for peace, happiness, and sunshine in the soul (no matter what!), sooner or later most people find a link between earth and heaven—some familiar object or experience that is a constant reminder that we are born for the hour and time in which we live and then we move on to the next eternal phase.

Where our family lived, you see, heaven was just around the corner, where there was no fear and where the peaceful, happy moments rolled. From birth I was reared just a few of Salt Lake City's long blocks from "the only true temple," as we called it. The magnificent six-spired structure was in the path of everything I did in those formative years. It was the very foundation of our family. From our earliest days we learned that Mother and Father had "courted" walking past the temple and that they would hide little boxes of candy to enjoy on the return trip. Dad unfailingly showed us the very spot where they hid their treasure. Later they were married inside that most beautiful building—it was the starting place of their family. It was the starting place of the families of each of their children, as well.

On a daily basis, the best part of any walk to anywhere was past the east side of the temple. Always we would stop, at least a moment, to peer through the mammoth, ornate wrought-iron gate to see what was happening on the temple grounds. Was someone polishing the oversized brass door-knob and escutcheon on the entrance that was used only by General Authorities? Was a statue being cleaned? Were there autumn leaves yet? Were the gardens being stripped nearly naked for winter? Had the "farm fertilizer" been spread about? (They didn't even plant pansies until spring in those days.) Or was it the season, at last, when the crocus braved late winter storms? Were the fruit trees blooming? We learned the variety of fruit trees by annually noting the timing and color of the blossoms—popcorn white for apricot, as the Primary song says. Later came peach blossoms against gnarled bark. But the apple trees were the prettiest, with baby green leaves clustered among white petals with pink hearts.

Whatever the season or situation, on a daily basis we walked right down Capitol Hill and past that beloved temple as we went shopping, to the library, to medical appointments and music and dance lessons, to Salt Lake Costume House in the Constitution Building to get costumes for endless productions. And there were the weekly movies at the nearby Paramount, Orpheum, and Capitol Theaters. The roller-skating rink owned by the father of my friend Larona was practically next door to our grade school, which was on the boundary street—North Temple—of the beloved wall enclosing Temple Square. President David O. McKay's son Robert was the best skater of all, and he added a certain panache to our little society in the Lafayette School District. The McKay home was right across the street from the north gate of the temple and was neighbor to the original Primary Children's Hospital.

One of President and Sister McKay's daughters was just enough older than I was that she seemed unusually glamorous to me. I watched her carefully, and everything she did was desirable. Her readings in the Tabernacle on holidays or celebrations were moving, with just the right sense of the dramatic. She was the closest thing to a celebrity or movie star in our midst. She was poised and ladylike and impressive. And she was in love with Conway Ashton. Those were Depression days, and Temple Square was the setting for many fine firesides, musical options, and pageants. The young couples courting had no money to spend and few places to go that were free, so they'd go to the programs on Temple Square, and afterward they would walk around and around that temple block like Joshua's troops. Sometimes they'd stop to dream their dreams as they gazed up at the mysterious, promising temple from the corner of North Temple and Main Streets. When Emma Rae and her Conway finally gave up gazing and realized their dreams of being married in the temple, I knew that was what I wanted to do someday too.

We never *played* on Temple Square, but we spent a good deal of time there. We haunted the old museum full of Egyptian mummies, pioneer handcarts, and Indian relics including peace pipes and beaded moccasins. We studied the portraits of the old prophets as if to learn the secret of their longevity if not their goodness. We sat on the east steps of the fat, beetle-shaped Tabernacle to study the angel Moroni, which was the nearest thing to heaven on our own turf. I was especially fascinated with the symbolic clasped hands carved in the granite walls of the temple. Mother had taught me that those hands had been carved by one of our ancestors, so that gave me an edge until one of my friends' mothers became a temple ordinance worker and served inside that building.

During my West High School years the temple was still a vital *place* in my life. We hung around the square on conference Sunday, mostly for the social connections it gave us. We often took a "shortcut" from the school through Temple Square to ZCMI to buy supplies for the school assembly, prom, team, athletic rally, or classroom project. Such gladness in a safe and happy youth enhanced by the places sacred to our Church growth and culture!

We never took for granted Temple Square with its centerpiece, the temple, that pristine palace of dreams. Our horizons were stretched as we listened to the great organ and watched the Native Americans with blankets and even wigwams on the grounds at general conference. We eavesdropped among the visiting foreigners, trying to detect their nationalities by their strange languages. We were fascinated by the magic of snowflakes filigreed in the special lighting about the temple spires at night.

During the blackout days of World War II the temple stood in holy darkness, a symbol of our grief for loved ones lost as well as for missed opportunities, limitations, the stifling of sacred feelings during war. Yet, with the guidance of parents and teachers, we knew the light of the Lord was shining within those thick granite blocks. We *knew* it and took hope.

More years later there came the Christmas with million upon million of strings of lights up and down twig and branch, along metal railings, marking path and crèche display. It was a fairyland, a bit of heaven on earth. It became a gathering place for families seeking a higher celebration of the season.

Until I was married there, I had only been inside the portion of the temple where the baptismal font rested on the backs of twelve huge, bronzed sculpted oxen that seemed much bigger and higher and grander than in life. We were impressed with the information that a similar setting had existed in ancient times in King Solomon's Temple. We children who had been baptized ourselves were now able to do baptisms for those who had not been baptized while here on earth. *Vicarious* was an early vocabulary triumph! We were doing *vicarious* work—being baptized for those who couldn't do it for themselves. We would deliciously count the number of people for whom we were immersed or "buried" under the water. *Immersed* was another strange word with which we became familiar. We learned what it meant (totally covered with water) and how to spell it, much as other school children learned to chant, "*M-i*-double *s-i*-double *s-i*-double *p-i*."

As a young woman my focus was on the living, not the dead. Passing by I would study the temple's slender windows—two stories tall, richly trimmed with layers and levels of thick molding curving into a graceful arch at the top—with folds of fragile fabric giving privacy to the ceremonies being performed inside.

At different times during my college days I worked in the Society Department for each of the newspapers in Salt Lake.

My job was to follow the weddings. For the pictures, I'd wipe lipstick from the groom's mouth and give the bride's train a professional flip, slowly easing it back to the floor so that the folds of fabric wrapped about her legs just so and swirled in front as she posed. I went to the Greek Orthodox church, the synagogue, the Country Club, the University of Utah sorority houses, Memorial House in Memory Grove in City Creek Canyon; I went to the small cottages and Protestant churches as well as the cathedrals. In every case there was a radiant bride and an excited bridegroom, eager to get on with the proceedings. And there was love there.

Later, during my senior year at the University of Utah, I was hired as the editor of the Society and Women's Department of the *Deseret News.* I had been married four days when this job started. My wedding was much like all the countless others I had written about as a cub society reporter. The one big difference was that now I had a broader comparison. Now I had been inside the holy temple! As in the other places I had been for wedding assignments, in the temple on my wedding day there was a radiant bride and an excited groom. As in the other places, love was felt there. Parents wept.

But there was more! I sensed something that was *not* part of the other marriages in other locations that I had reported on. In the temple there was the power of God, the presence of the Holy Spirit, the promise of marriage "for time and all eternity." And such promises of God's blessings as I'd never imagined! Such gladness!

Later I learned that this wasn't a remarkable temple wedding just because it was *my* wedding. Since that day I have attended countless temple marriages. The incredible sweetening of the event by the Holy Spirit sets these weddings apart from all others. It is a feeling that cannot be matched by all the anthems or recessionals; the flowers, ribbons, candles, and love birds; the elaborate gowns on bridesmaids and flower girls. These things are not part of the temple wedding ceremony, but so hallowed is the circumstance they are not even missed.

A Latter-day Saint temple is a busy place. There is always a variety of activities under way, all of them relative to the eternal well-being of Heavenly Father's children. Yet, with all of the people and procedures, there is no confusion; rather there is a mellowing tranquility. Everyone is dressed in special all-white clothing worn only inside the temple. There is something else about the white clothing—people are the same, equal. It is not a fashion show of personal preference, of financial success, of trends. Across the world in the house of the Lord there is no delineation of status, race, culture, or personal accomplishment. No one is a celebrity, and no one is labeled a poor, pitiful person.

In order to enter the temple, people have to be worthy. They must have a recommend, which they receive following personal interviews with a bishopric member and a member of the stake presidency. And because there is purity of standards and purpose, in the temple the Holy Ghost abides. It is felt. People have a desire to participate in the work of God's kingdom on earth, which prepares them for the kingdom of heaven someday.

For example, our extended family had moved forward with doing the necessary temple work for my father's brother who had married out of the Church and been inactive all the rest of his life. He died when he was close to ninety years old, some years after my father died. We knew our responsibility to this good man and to our father, who desired that his brother's temple work be done. First, the personal endowment for Uncle had to be performed. My brother was to be proxy in that ordinance. He is a busy professional, and the appointed day proved crammed with crises at his workplace. He had fasted, but he had not had time to meditate or prayerfully seek the Spirit of the Lord. At last he rushed into the temple and quickly dressed in his white clothing. If only it were as simple to cast off the outside world and get in the mood of the experience ahead as it was to change clothing. In his dressing room cubicle, my brother bowed his head and earnestly prayed to have the spirit of peace and to be able to focus on the sacred work he had come to do. Before he closed his prayer he humbly asked Heavenly Father to witness to him whether this effort was going to be important to our beloved deceased uncle. Immediately my brother was touched with a gentle warmth in his heart that soon flooded his whole being, and he knew he had an answer to his prayer. It *did* matter to Uncle. The ceremony he would participate in for Uncle was important to that beloved man, gone from this earth now. The work was true!

There are many instances of links between people who have passed on without their temple work being accomplished and those on earth doing the work. For example, a fine, gentle Englishman came up to me following a Church meeting where I was visiting and asked, "Do you remember being in the London Temple in the fall of 1962?" When I assured him that I did, he asked me if I could recall anything special about the sealing session I had participated in at that time. I was startled because I hadn't recognized him at first. However, through his question I knew who he was, if not his name. This man was the only other person who could have known about the special thing that happened.

Background: a group of Church leaders were traveling to give training sessions for local members in England. The London Temple president, Selvoy Boyer, arranged for our party to do some sealings, and there were several local Saints invited to join with us.

It was on this occasion that the English gentleman that I referred to and I were proxy at the altar for three different deceased couples. Each couple was sealed as man and wife—the English stranger acting proxy for each husband and I standing in for each wife. He and I had never met each other before. The special thing that happened was that as the second couple was sealed together for time and for all eternity, each of us felt a strong, warm feeling surging through us. We did not feel this for the first couple nor the third. Later we spoke only to each other about the experience—and rather shyly, wondering if the other one had felt this remarkable manifestation of the Spirit. It was the same for him as for me. We didn't see each other again until the evening, many years later, when he approached me following the meeting. Neither of us had forgotten the witness of the Spirit that the work we did that day was for a couple who was waiting for it on the other side of the veil! Of this there was no doubt in either of us.

The work of the Lord and the inevitable gladness and incomprehensible joy it brings will continue to fill more and more hearts. When our children and our grandchildren, and others we love who may not be in our immediate line, begin to be gathered together forever, then will the peaceful, happy moments roll and sunshine flood our hearts.

4

Hope and Praise and Love

Gladness! Joy! Fulfillment! These feelings are magnified in a holy temple. For Latter-day Saints the temple is the highlight of life's experiences.

Elder James E. Talmage spoke of the temple: "No jot, iota, or tittle of the temple rites is otherwise than uplifting and sanctifying. In every detail the endowment ceremony contributes to covenants of morality of life, consecration of person to high ideals, devotion to truth, patriotism to nation, and allegiance to God." (*The House of the Lord* [Salt Lake City: Deseret Book Co., 1976], p. 84.)

During an area conference in Korea I sat on the stand, wrapped in new blankets against the Korean cold, looking out upon the faithful, spiritually hungry, deeply thrilled Latter-day Saints who had gathered there. There was a rich lifting of the spirit just to be in the company of President Spencer W. Kimball. President Gordon B. Hinckley counseled the people of Korea to increase their faithful effort to turn their country from its war-torn evil and agony to a place where the Spirit of God could dwell. He promised that in return for such obedience and faithfulness the people would have a temple! There was a great stir among the people. What joy! It seemed impossible for such a miracle to occur in the near future. Yet, just a few years later they had their temple.

A shopkeeper and his wife had asked us questions about our visit to their country. The conversation went so well that we invited them to come to the meeting at the mission home that evening. Immediately they phoned to make arrangements with their maid to take care of their two little children. She was willing to stay through the evening, so they came to the informal gathering. The talk centered around hope for a temple in their country someday. This young couple was seeking truth, and the stirrings inside of them were heightened by the local people at the gathering as they talked about a *temple* and *eternal marriage* and *forever families*. They were thrilled at the promise of a "sacred celebration," as they called it, that they could prepare for that would bind them together forever with their children. A flood of converts came into the Church following the visit of a prophet of the Lord.

In April 1974 at general conference, Elder Gordon B. Hinckley related a story from New Zealand concerning the sacrifices people will make for the temple experience: "I remember hearing in New Zealand the testimony of a man from the far side of Australia who, having been previously married by civil authority and then joined the Church with his wife and children, had traveled all the way across that wide continent, then across the Tasman Sea to Auckland, and down to the temple in the beautiful valley of the Waikata. As I remember his words, he said, 'We could not afford to come. Our worldly possessions consisted of an old car, our furniture, and our dishes. I said to my family, "We cannot afford to go." Then I looked into the faces of my beautiful wife and our beautiful children, and I said, "We cannot afford *not* to go. If the Lord will give me strength, I can work and earn enough for another car and furniture and dishes, but if I should lose these my loved ones, I would be poor indeed in both life and in eternity." '" ("The Marriage That Endures," *Ensign,* May 1974, p. 24.)

In Brazil, President Teofilo Puertas took our party of Church leaders on a private tour of the São Paulo Temple. This spiritual giant looked the part of a temple president and caretaker of the house of the Lord. He was handsome, white haired, and radiant from some inner light earned through devotion to the Lord and the work of the kingdom of God on earth.

Apparently we weren't the only ones to think so.

A family from a small village had come to the temple to be sealed together. In preparation for the event, they had taught their children about the sanctity of the temple and how they must be clean and pure to enter it because this sacred building was Heavenly Father's house and his Spirit could be felt there.

When the family arrived the little boy came up to President Puertas and looked at him in wonder and adoration. As I recall, the conversation went something like this:

"Are you Heavenly Father?" the boy asked.

President Puertas was surprised but sensitive to the excitement in the little fellow. "No, but I am his son," he said. "And so are you—a child of God!"

Then President Puertas smiled and patted the boy on the head. It was a warm and wonderful moment of truth.

Qualifying for temple participation has its parallels in life sometimes. My husband and I had gone to northern California for the dedication of the Oakland Temple. President David O. McKay was presiding. Along the approach to the temple we had to show our tickets to various ushers along the path, who then directed us to the next "checkpoint." Each time we showed our tickets we were delighted as we were directed ever closer to the temple itself, instead of to an overflow facility. Finally we came through the door of the very room where the First Presidency and other General Authorities and their wives were gathering. It was beautiful. Marvelous. We'd made it!

As we waited to be seated, our tickets were checked once again. This time the kind usher said to us, "Oh, I'm sorry. Your seating is in the next room." And he showed us how to get there. We tried to be humble and accepting and not weep from disappointment as we moved to the next room. Oh, we could see the Church leaders, and we breathed the same air in the same building. We looked upon their backs and heard their voices over the speaker system. But . . . we . . . were . . . not . . . in . . . their . . . presence!

This was truly sobering. We sensed how dreadful it would be, through some small neglect of worthiness, to be relegated to a lower kingdom in heaven. We vowed a vow to live so that we would not be disappointed on Judgment Day!

The dedication of the Seattle Temple in November 1980 stirred considerable public demonstration. As we drove up the private driveway for the dedication ceremony, we pitied the disgruntled, albeit misguided, women who had chained themselves to the temple gates in protest of women's inequality. There were also other kinds of outbursts by helpers in the adversary's determined effort to thwart the work of the Lord.

Inside, during the meeting, it was dramatic to hear Elder Boyd K. Packer quote President Brigham Young. Elder Packer said, "When the Saints arrived in the Salt Lake Valley, Brigham Young, in his first act, planted his cane and said, 'Here we will build a temple to our God.' Later when he announced that the work was to proceed, there were many tears in the valley, ostensively tears of joy, but they were bittersweet tears, for the Saints knew from experience, as Brigham Young said, 'we never began to build a temple without the bells of hell beginning to ring.' And then he said, 'I want to hear them ring again.'" Elder Packer reminded us that the Saints knew of the persecution that would come, for they had been driven away from Kirtland. Then, in Independence, persecution and opposition had erupted as soon as the temple was started. In Far West it was repeated. In Nauvoo opposition to the building of the temple ended with the temple in flames and the Saints finally moving west. Said Elder Packer, "Those who had taken the temples had nothing. Our forebears had with them the keys." (Elder Boyd K. Packer, Seattle Temple dedication, 1:30 p.m., Monday, November 17, 1980.)

One of the most glorious moments in any temple was the dedication of the Tokyo Temple on 27 October 1980. Priesthood leaders had come from the Asian area stakes that were in the temple district at that time. The group included people from Taiwan, Korea, Hong Kong, the Philippines. There were two aspects of this gathering that added to the emotion and ultimately to the spirit of this temple dedication. First, because of political impositions couples were not allowed to leave the country together. Therefore, some of the wives were not given visas from these nations to accompany their spouses to Japan. The second component of this drama was the fact that the countries represented there in the Tokyo Temple District had been enemies—at one time or another engaged in bitter war. Of course, that included those of us who were leaders from Church headquarters, from the United States of America, a country which had been at war with Japan, Vietnam, and North Korea.

Elder Gordon B. Hinckley said the people there were "witnesses of the miracle" that had begun seventy-nine years earlier in 1901 when Elder Heber J. Grant dedicated Japan for the flourishing of the gospel. It is no wonder that President Dwayne N. Anderson called the Tokyo Temple dedication "the most important event in the history of Asia." President Spencer W. Kimball presided, and at the first session he welcomed members to "one of the most significant events that have occurred in the Church, the dedication of this lovely building to the Lord."

It was announced that the opening prayer would be offered by In Sang Han from Korea. At that time he was not yet a member of the Seventy. Brother Han was a humble man who had suffered greatly at the hand of enemies during his country's conflicts. Now former political enemies were gathered as brothers and sisters in the sacred house of the Lord for a purpose far surpassing the problems of the world. Brother Han stood as a symbol of this healing spirit that we felt. His voice choked with emotion and humility at being voice for the various nationalities represented there. He was flooded with emotion and a witness from the Holy Ghost, and tears flowed freely down his cheeks. Soon everyone was weeping. There were audible sobs. There swept over us the strong power of the Holy Spirit, and we became aware of an exuberant gratitude for God's goodness to his children everywhere and for all that was now enjoyed—for all power and wholesomeness that were available through the gospel of Jesus Christ and for the opportunities that the institution of the Church provided.

Mary Ellen Edmunds has written about an experience she had with a woman she met during her missionary travels in the Orient: "A dear sister who lived in very humble circum-stances once said to me, 'Sister, we're going to be able to go to the temple!' I couldn't think of any way to respond, be-cause I couldn't imagine how they'd be able to accomplish such a goal; the closest temple was being built in Tokyo. Then she said, 'If we sell everything in our home we don't need . . .' My mind quickly took me through their humble home, which I had visited several times. I wondered what they were going to sell that they didn't need. '. . . And if we save every Rupiah we can, we'll be able to go to the temple in fifty-five years!' I felt a lump in my throat and couldn't have responded even if I had thought of something to say. Then she added, 'Oh, Sister, I hope we'll still be alive—we'll be 110 years old.' As I write this, I'm able to look out my office window and see the Provo Temple." ("'The People Have Given Me a New Heart,'" *Ensign,* September 1982, p. 17.)

Robert and Suzanne Winston have had extensive experi-ence in Church service. They presided over the Atlanta Georgia Temple, and they currently serve in the presidency of the St. George Temple. They have had interesting experiences with the Saints who prepare for the choice opportunity of at-tending the temple. President Winston said: "There are many sidelights to our work. Recently, for example, I had a call from a young BYU student, the son of some people we had known in Florida, who asked if I could perform his marriage in the St. George Temple. I replied that I would be happy to do so, and then he said, 'By the way, can we also use your cabin for our honeymoon?'" President Winston reported to us that in the couple's thank-you note, they said they had enjoyed a "sensa-tional" time in the cabin even though it rained or snowed in the mountains every day. Humorously, President Winston commented that perhaps they could now boost the temple's statistics by offering package deals—marriage ceremony plus a honeymoon house—to anyone who would consent to mar-riage in the St. George Temple!

Donald S. Conkey, who with his wife, Joan, serves in the baptistry of the Atlanta Georgia Temple, reported that fifteen youth from Oxford, Mississippi, spent their spring break trav-eling several hundred miles to the temple to do baptisms for the dead. Brother Conkey said: "One of these was a young man who had been blind since birth, never seeing form or color. As I looked at this special child of God, I wondered how I could convey to him the beauty of the chapel and the baptistry, so he could take the images of these rooms with him."

As the baptismal work took place Brother Conkey pondered the possibilities. After the service he called upon a twelve-year-old young man, a first-time visitor to the temple, to describe the paintings. "As we listened to this twelve-year-old describe in minute detail the painting of Christ being baptized by John the Baptist, the painting came alive for all of us. A reverent hush fell on all in the baptistry, and tears flowed as we listened to a youth wise beyond his age convey to a blind companion the beauty of the pictures . . . communicating as only the Spirit can direct." I have thought many times since then about how much is missed by people who do not avail themselves of the temple experience.

When the Jordan River Temple in the south end of the Salt Lake Valley was dedicated, Jeneal Taylor was an employee of the ZCMI store in the Cottonwood Mall. She was in fashion accessories and enjoyed the many women who came to the department to purchase special white handkerchiefs for the Hosanna Shout. She said: "Several women told me they were buying their hankies a month in advance. They were going to keep them on their dressers to remind them to prepare themselves spiritually each day. One sweet lady told me that her husband had died right after her fourth child was born. She cleaned house for a living, and going to the temple dedication was tremendously exciting and meaningful for her. I could tell by looking at her that she didn't have much in the way of worldly means, but she seemed to be a very happy person. . . . Our hankies ranged from $2.60 on up to about $40.00. . . . She chose the one she liked best. She kept feeling it and looking at it. She asked how much it was, and I reluctantly told her $15.00. She said, 'This is the one I'm going to buy,' as she took the $15.00 hankie. She told me that she has her temple clothes in a little suitcase, ready for her burial someday. She said that because her family were not members of the Church they wouldn't know how to dress her for burial, so she has this special case with her clothes ready in it.

" 'After the dedication I am going to put this hankie with it and my whole outfit will be complete,' she said. She thanked me for waiting on her, and as I started to ring up the hankie, she pulled from out of her purse a little white envelope in which she kept her money. After we finished the transaction, I put the hankie in a sack and watched her walk away with it as if it were a pound of gold!"

Elder Harold B. Lee said: "When you enter a holy temple, you are by that course gaining fellowship with the Saints in God's eternal kingdom, where time is no more. In the temples of your God you are endowed not with a rich legacy of worldly treasure, but with a wealth of eternal riches that are above price.

"The temple ceremonies are designed by a wise Heavenly Father who has revealed them to us in these last days as a guide and a protection throughout our lives, that you and I might not fail to merit exaltation in the celestial kingdom where God and Christ dwell." ("Enter a Holy Temple," *Improvement Era,* June 1967, p. 144.)

The work that we do when we enter the temple transcends anything that takes place outside its walls. It is an experience that should not be limited to being vicariously enjoyed by hearing others talk about it. The keys to eternity and the gladness of being part of a bit of heaven on earth are available to any person who becomes prepared for entry inside the sacred walls of a temple in that person's part of the world.

The work of the Lord and the inevitable gladness and incomprehensible joy connected with it will continue to fill more and more hearts!

5

Sunshine, Blessed Sunshine

Caution! Medical science has issued a startling warning—there is an outbreak of diphtheria and tuberculosis abroad in the land. What if there were an outbreak of random acts of gladness in society, instead? Oh, the sunshine, the blessed sunshine we'd enjoy then!

Some people hate winter with its leafless trees and naked fields, while others see scenes of exquisite monotones with dark twigs and fence posts etched against the frost. It's all in the way one looks at it. So is life. It is mostly grim or mostly glad, depending on what soul is appraising it.

Imagine the spread of happy contagion if people focused on all the wonderful things that have happened to them in a week or a lifetime. More than blessing-counting, this could be a remembrance of happenings that set your heart to pounding and caused your shoulders to relax, your arms to fold about you, your eyes to glisten with tears, your voice to soften.

Enough of negativism! There has been too much recounting of trials and highlighting of personal martyrdom. On with remembering that life is about gladness, too. Yes!

Find the joy!

Just think, if people began a campaign of glad tidings they could make "blessed sunshine" The Trend.

Now, before doubt stifles your smile, rest assured that it

can be done, because it has been done! Start small and think *epidemic* of gladness, goodness, blessed sunshine.

A group of neighbor women of all ages and stations—women with all kinds of problems, hassles, responsibilities, disappointments, and ailments in life—went on an overnight retreat. It was to be a spring break. It turned out to be a gathering of gladness. Lee Yates stood before them and keynoted a sharing time by revealing three or four moments of joy in her own life. Among other things she told of the inevitable, warm fluttering of her heart when she heard her husband's footsteps in the hall at the end of the day. The unique rhythm to his slow, steady walk not only still moved her after more than twenty years but rendered her weak with joy. No matter what the day had brought, no matter the devastating surprises and demanding stresses, he was home! Everything would be all right. He was her safe haven. As Lee said, she knew from long experience that Bob would "absorb and lighten her worries."

It was contagious, this positive rehearsal of selective vignettes. The women in this group either nodded in agreement or caught the spirit and volunteered their own high points of happiness. Afterward, the epidemic of gladness lasted for days and spread across town in the kitchens, cafes, shopping lines, and bedrooms of their community. It was good to be so happily *infected*.

This is the kind of glad happening that the war-weary world needs. It could be on a par with Pierre Teilhard de Chardin's comment on love: "Some day, after we have mastered the winds, the waves, the tides, and gravity, we shall harness the energies of love. Then for the second time in the history of the world, man will have discovered fire." Discovering the fire of love is good. How about flooding the earth for the second time—in a sea of rejoicing one with another about life's wonderful moments?

How about scattering some sunshine?

When was your last happy time?

What moment of joy stands out in your whole life?

What have you done that delighted someone, surprised them with joy?

Janet Lee, first lady of Brigham Young University and wife of President Rex Lee, once said during a women's conference on campus that "life doesn't have to be perfect to be perfectly wonderful." She suggested keeping a catalogue of moments of joy for future reveling in.

As a career homemaker with the forever-burden of a journalist's deadline "on the side," I clearly recall the absolute thrill, one magic night, of awakening to the perfect wonder of my world—having tons of laundry et al., yes, but also being mother to six very young, very normal but precious children who had been lent to us for a season by Heavenly Father. As usual I was bone tired, not darling, not very alert but full of duty still as I checked each sleeping little one. Each received a tuck of the blanket, a kiss on the forehead, and a whispered promise into a small ear, "I am glad you are mine!" Susan, age three, stirred and sleepily responded with limp arms lifted for a hug. Then she mumbled, "You *are?* Me, too!"

It was a significant connection between spirits—mine, hers, and God's—much like the one made by the woman who touched the Savior's garment and was healed and he *knew* that "virtue had gone out of him" and that a significant connection had been made.

I had ridden to the airport in Manila, Philippines, with my husband, who was on his way home. Because of typhoon warnings, it was doubtful whether he'd be able to take off. My driver and I watched the plane lift into the air just before the airport closed. By the time I was safely in my room on the twenty-second floor of the Manila Peninsula Hotel, the typhoon was raging like nothing I had ever experienced before and I was frightened. The power was out. The palm trees were horizontal in the flooding streets. When it was too dark to see anymore, except for flashes of lightening, I climbed into bed. I had never, ever felt more alone. I literally pledged my hand into God's and reverted to my childhood prayer-poem, "Now I lay me down to sleep, I pray thee, Lord, my soul to keep. If I should die before I wake, I pray thee, Lord, my soul to take."

In the morning, destruction was everywhere, and no sunshine. My top feeling was gratitude that I was alive and that the elevator was working so I could make it down to the lobby. I was in a sensitive, sober mood as I waited to keep an appointment with my driver to take me to the war memorial of the casualties of the Pacific theater, World War II. He was late but was willing to drive me to the sacred, deeply impressive place. It was my first time there, so though it was pouring rain, I wandered alone beneath the tall arches so I could scan panel after panel of thousands of names for the names of my friends who had fallen in the line of duty. There were many, of course, because it was, after all, *our* war. Then I found the name of a boy I had known well since childhood. Long years ago I had danced with him to the big bands, exchanged little gifts, and indulged in long phone calls. When I found his name I was surprised at my reaction. Suddenly my tears were a match for the weather. I was not prepared for the enveloping of the Spirit I felt at that moment. I lifted my face to the weeping wind and gave in to solemn grief. Yet I felt gratitude in the memories. In spite of the turn life had taken, we had had one wonderful time as lighthearted youth.

My driver had been watching me and came to my rescue with an enormous black umbrella. He'd seen others go through this experience. He was a fine, typically poverty-stricken Filipino who lived with his wife and several children in a community where the pitiful homes were made of packing boxes used in shipping. The typhoon had flattened their home. Crude as it had been, it was all that they had had. My driver explained this and said it was the reason he was late for our appointment that morning. He had been helping to unload new packing boxes delivered to the site so people could rebuild their shelters. And I realized he'd taken time off from that work just to indulge some American lady!

Joy came in suddenly understanding God's statement regarding the worth of souls, and in recognizing the quality of God's children and the contribution strangers make to strangers whether in war or heartbreak.

On occasion a whole crowd can be glad. Like when the young women of the Church prepared their written testimonies, tucked them into helium-filled balloons, and en masse, worldwide according to plan, released them to float skyward before falling into the hands of someone who could benefit from such sweet sentiment. Reports from the day's event were unanimous from one continent to another that just being part of the event was an impressive piece of happiness to these teenagers with high hopes.

Speaking of balloons, we took some little children along with our own to the state fair. At the end of our adventure, we splurged and bought each one the balloon they'd begged for. This balloon was tied around his or her wrist to keep it from slipping away into the air unscheduled. We made it through the exit gates without incident, but then a little girl nervously scratched her wrist where the balloon string was tied. That loosened the knot and away floated that big yellow balloon before anything could be done about it. Her tears were sudden. Her anguish was reflected in her wails. Though *we* could not comfort her, a little boy's quick, unselfish gesture did. He untied his own balloon string and let his balloon go free toward the white clouds. "See," he cried to the unhappy little girl. "See, my balloon is chasing yours. It's bea-u-tiful! Look!" Everybody looked. Soon they all released their balloons in a parade of flying color. They were delighted, excited, elated, agog, and surprised by a kind of fun they'd never had before. It was the turning of trauma into gladness. It was a better idea than taking those balloons home to wilt or pop, or to squeak Dad into fits. Honestly, it is one of my most jubilant memories.

Through random acts of gladness we see the variance possible in our joy. A single incident can be greater than the sum of its parts because of how it strikes us at the time. It doesn't have to be particularly spiritual, but it must touch the spirit. It may be something as simple as a surprising compliment when it is needed most, a lesson well given through the power of the Holy Ghost, a baby's first tooth, an immediate answer to prayer such as when a lost diamond ring is found or the car starts when you are stalled in traffic. Or perhaps you see a former love unexpectedly, and it is like Paul Engle's snowflake on the palm of your hand in mid-July.

There is an ever-so-slight nuance of gladness that sensitive people discern in certain circumstances. This sensitivity makes a difference in whether joy is felt or altogether missed. It has to do with personal preparation or experience that heightens one's response. Dreams. Expectations. Values. Gospel orientation. Time frame.

Gladness comes with the deliberate remembering of a joyful time. When you make a record of it, it can be reread, replayed, relived. And forever remembered. It may even start a Trend.

6

Passing On the Sunshine

The emergency room, a call to 911, the Heimlich maneuver, plus all manner of medical procedures and potions often extend a life without maintaining or improving its quality. Critical physical problems are a plague in the midst of scientific advance. "No place to go," "no room at the inn," and "no funds or financing" are desperate cries of people needing care—cries that remain unheard as mansions encroach on the foothills, canyons, and skies in every community.

What is needed here is someone to shoulder the burden, highlight the blessings, and pass on the sunshine!

"I can't deal with this!" is often the confession of a frustrated family member thrust into a new role of caring for others: grandchildren moving in, a teenage son forever injured in a motorcycle accident, a grandpa who lives (*exists* may be a better word) to a very *ripe* old age, an in-law who has suffered a stroke, a widowed mother, a wife with cancer. Whatever the situation, they need help! These who are too infirm or too troubled to care for themselves become the object and the symbol of the "test of our time."

But there are others who need to be saved, helped, and caught up in the "gathering" of Heavenly Father's choice children. There are people who have never learned the gospel; there are children who are abandoned or orphaned. These

47

people need such nurturing. Too many people who live in reconstituted families or who are jolted into a different work or worship situation ache for a comforting word of acceptance as they struggle to find their place.

What is needed here is someone to share the glad tidings, to turn on the light, to open the shades to sunshine.

Enter the Caregiver.

If they will and if they are able to, caregivers, care agencies, unselfish families, and sensitive associates can make the difference for life's desolate victims of one thing or another. Caregivers come in assorted sizes, shapes, and ages, and they may be of either gender. They have one thing in common: they understand that life can be bright . . . *anyway!* Enduring to the end—or until this sequence is over—doesn't have to be a jaw-clenching, molar-gritting existence of quiet desperation.

Consider caregiver Johanna. She was only twelve when she was thrust into this role, but her heart was prepared by living close to Christ. That was the wonder of Johanna. Johanna was twelve when Megan moved into her neighborhood. Megan's mother had just died and so this thirteen-year-old girl was immediately thrust into the care and keeping of the father who had divorced her mother and married another woman when Megan was a toddler. The stress Megan felt in these circumstances was breaking her. Her whole life and environment had totally changed. Everything was drastically different: family lifestyle, city, neighborhood, house, bedroom, ward and Young Women class, school, doctors. There were so many changes in her life that missing her mother's love and guidance could not even be reckoned with. Megan even was denied closeness with her mother's family, who had played such a vital part in her life, particularly in the recent past while her mother was ill and dying.

Then Megan met Johanna. What a sunbeam she was! During this critical period, Johanna was an angel-of-mercy friend.

The burden of such a friendship is not easy. There are inevitable impositions from confused emotions, insecurities and immaturity, even parental misunderstandings. But Johanna kept close. She listened, comforted, planned small surprises, and with the generous help of her parents, invited Megan to share in sleepovers, family prayers, and discussions that deeply influenced her and blessed her life. Johanna was a caregiver at her young age.

Every story of people helping people is different. For example, during World War II my husband was stationed at United States Military Hospital in Brigham City, Utah. He was trained and assigned as staff director for the education rehabilitation of the patients who had been wounded in the war. At the hospital Italian and German prisoners of war became the maintenance crew of the vast complex of buildings and grounds. It was plush duty for them to be in such a setting, even though they were under guard. This was a period of incredible turnaround in medicine and human relationships. Charity abounded, even while heartbreak was everywhere. Friends and family often were viewed as enemies while strangers reversed tragedy. One day in the glassed foyer of the headquarters building, I witnessed such a phenomenon.

A taxi stopped in front of the building, and a young woman got out of the cab and talked with the driver for a moment before starting her walk to the entrance. She was about halfway to the hospital, when she turned around and darted back to the waiting taxi. The car made a U-turn to continue back down the street. Suddenly it stopped to park across the street opposite the hospital. Again the young woman stepped from the cab, crossed the street, and slowly started the long walk to the main entrance. Intermittently she'd pause, drop her chin to her chest, look back at the cab, look over toward the hospital—thinking, thinking, weighing it all.

Being an incurable romantic, I watched the proceedings with interest. By the time the young woman made her second approach, I was praying for her positive progress into the building. You see, beside me in the foyer, in his wheelchair, was an attractive soldier with both legs amputated (or blown off in the line of duty). He was waiting and watching, too. This young woman held his future happiness in the warmth of her heart, and she was vacillating!

Almost there . . . then abruptly she stopped again. She shook her head a moment before turning to run back to the still-waiting taxi. You see, this wasn't the first time that the cabbie had been through this routine of delivering visitors from great distances for a reunion with a loved one in the hospital.

Some went through with it and some backed off. Some simply could not face the ravages of war and the resulting imposition that would become a part of their own life, and the serviceman-patient was left to find other comfort sources.

The last time the girl started toward the hospital, she abruptly turned and got into the taxi, and it pulled away from the curb, picking up speed. I felt sick and helpless as the soldier's head slumped forward in despair. Then he rolled his wheelchair about and slowly started down the long hospital hall back to his quarters.

The German prisoners of war, as if on command, backed up against the windows they had been cleaning and formed a kind of attentive, respectful honor guard of caregivers for the sobbing soldier to wheel through. One of them started a rousing German song, and soon they all blended their voices in the soldier's behalf. Then the young soldier lifted his tear-stained face and began bumping his wheelchair into the zigzag pattern that signified, "Who, me? Hey, I am going to be OK!"

Those enemy prisoners of war who passed on the sunshine recognized courage, and to a man they applauded the paraplegic until he turned the corner.

Cynthia Vale Benson, wife of Alva, was a caregiver in a unique way. She lived in early times in Cedar City, Utah—a bleak place in its pioneering period. Every spring big floods poured down Cedar Canyon, carrying silt and mud to deposit about the dwellings. But Cynthia was a caregiver of her community. Determined to do her part to make this an attractive place to live, she used the desert pink silt mud to paint her windowsills and door frames so that her house looked lived in, valued, and cared for. Others quickly followed suit.

Our three-year-old son appointed himself to be his dad's caregiver when his dad suffered a concussion. Tirelessly the boy spent every waking moment sitting by his dad's bed, singing songs and telling his own creative stories. He did errand duty, and was the chief planner of such distracting surprises as a daily costume parade and show-and-tell-please-get-well sessions with pictures hand drawn or torn from magazines.

He also did imitations of visitors who came, which the whole family enjoyed. Laughter cooled dismay and hastened healing in a frightened family.

Assigning home teachers as representatives of the local bishop to visit in a home is a magnificent plan. In a similar vein, the Relief Society's visiting teaching program is an organized means whereby the women of the Church receive regular instructional and charitable visits from their ward sisters. The visiting teachers note needs, which aren't always temporal, and they build the security of belonging. They are to lift and fortify the sisters they visit, as well as give them a gospel message, and in this way help there to be joy and gladness in ever-increasing measure in the homes.

I had a visiting teacher who was a very important and very busy woman, yet she was a caregiver not only by assignment but because of the warmth of her heart. "I am your visiting teacher," she would say. "You *have* to let me help you!" She regularly placed by our door surprises—a big grapefruit, an avocado, her special bean casserole, or a scripture to inspire the mood of the day. On a very "big" birthday of mine she shared a news clipping that contained the slogan, "The sun setting is no less beautiful than the sun rising." Looking at her I could believe that.

Advancing age isn't a factor in caregiving on the receiving end only. It is a time of life when relationships can be sweeter than ever before. Surely you have noticed the magazine ad series, sponsored by Nuveen Investments, on the theme "the human bond." Watch for them, they are great. Couples who give to each other reach a point where, as the ad copy suggests, "he can go hours at a time without saying a word. And yet, she still knows exactly what he's thinking. It's something you have to experience to truly understand. If you have, no explanation is necessary. If you haven't, no explanation is possible." How right that is. I speak from personal experience.

Florida Scott-Maxwell was a gifted woman of letters and drama. Just before her death she wrote: "One cannot be honest even at the end of one's life, for no one is wholly alone. We are bound to those we love, or to those who love us, and to those who need us to be brave, or content, or even happy enough to allow them not to worry about us. So we must refrain from giving pain, as our last gift to our fellows. . . . When we are almost free of life we must retain guile that those still caught in life may not suffer more. The old must often try to be silent, if it is within their power, since silence may be like space, the intensely alive something that contains all. The clear echo of what we refrained from saying, every-thing, from the first pause of understanding, to the quiet of comprehension." (*The Measure of My Days* [New York: Alfred A. Knopf, 1968], pp. 142–43.) Even those who need caregivers can give care back in return by such a philosophical behavior.

Some years ago there was a magazine cartoon that comes to mind whenever someone near me has the flu or some other ailment that requires help from others in order for the person to get through the ordeal. The cartoon showed a rooster in bed, beneath a heap of covers. This domestic scene included an aproned hen standing beside the bed and holding a bowl and a spoon. The caption line was, "Keep still and eat your chicken soup!"

Oh, the irony!

A caregiver in today's world is more than one who dishes up chicken soup or presides over the passage from life to death, though none of us who have had experience with hos-pice or home health care personnel can overestimate their contribution under such circumstances. A caregiver, in another sense, helps those who are not going to die—yet! A caregiver improves the quality of life for someone regardless of what ails that person. Caregivers are not always related to their pa-tient—nor are they always even acquaintances—but often there is a remarkable bonding that develops between the needful and the caregiver.

Caregivers are something wonderful. They are in the sacred category of people helping people when they need it most. The appreciation felt for their efforts is almost overwhelming. Such feelings stir a sensitive soul to even higher sites—grati-tude for the inimitable watch care of Heavenly Father and for the facilitating benevolence of the Lord Jesus Christ.

Caregivers often do what no one else can, will, or wants to do. Caregivers work hard doing very unpleasant, even difficult, duties that are marked by a seeming sameness, bringing a kind of gladness to a desolate, broken, changed life. A caregiver can ease frustration, embarrassment in personal care, and the struggle for very basic emotional and physical needs and psychological perspective. A caregiver gives solace, sustenance, comfort, cleanliness, and cheer. Caregivers are hope as well as help.

Caregivers show up in unique situations. Some examples are shared here to prove the possibilities and the reach of people helping people in various ways—people who by so doing serve the Lord, as described in Matthew 25.

In Phoenix, Arizona, a family moved into a new home that had been vacated by a Latter-day Saint family. The previous owners didn't want to throw away their collection of Church magazines, so they left them neatly piled on a bench in the garage. These were found by the two daughters from the new family, and these girls began to read the magazines. The mother, being concerned about what her daughters were reading, leafed through the magazines and was impressed. She called her husband's attention to them, and together they read a number of the articles. They became so interested that they wrote a letter to Church headquarters in Salt Lake City, asking for more information about the Church. Soon they were taught and baptized, and they have declared themselves the happiest family in Arizona—or anyplace!

Another example was related in a Church magazine article: "A Church leader in an eastern city was approached by a little boy and asked to come to the boy's home, where his sister was seriously ill. Although he didn't know the boy, the older man responded immediately. He found the home to be a wretched one-room basement in a tenement. The mother had died, the father had disappeared, and the 15-year-old sister had carried on for the younger children. For almost a year she had been both breadwinner and mother, and now she lay in the terminal stages of a fatal disease.

"They talked that night of the future, of Heavenly Father's plan for his children, and of the joy that a homecoming would bring. . . . But one persistent question kept coming to her childlike mind:

" 'But *how?*' she asked. '*How* will he know that I belong to him?'

"As he prayed silently for help, the man received even as he gave. Looking down at the frail little creature, he saw on the ragged blanket the shriveled and work-worn fingers that had kept the dishes washed and the clothes ironed and the food cooked—fingers that by service and sacrifice had brought life to a little family.

" 'Show him your hands,' he said quietly. 'He'll know you belong to him.' " (Jeff Holland, "Show Him Your Hands," Era of Youth section, *Improvement Era,* October 1967, p. 39.)

Michael was a hairstylist. He had a devoted clientele not only because he was skilled in his profession so that he sent his clients forth looking beautiful but also because they left full of comfort on account of Michael's listening, caring, and gentle counseling. He was resourceful in time of a client's crisis. He'd turn a hospital room into a temporary salon. He was invited to funeral parlors to do the hair of clients who had died.

With great compassion Michael helped my friend Marie endure a very grimy divorce. Her humiliation in rejection, her deprivation of love, and the absence of a father figure for two children were one thing, but to starve was quite another. Marie was forced to go on Church welfare.

At the beauty salon the first week, Marie told Michael that she would not be coming to him for hair care for a while because she couldn't afford to pay him. To prove her point she told him about being forced onto Church welfare through another demeaning act of her husband.

"I love Deseret canned peaches," Michael said. "I'll do your hair for one can of peaches until once again you can pay me."

From then on Marie became known as "Peaches," even in the appointment ledger ten years later! In turn she dubbed her stylist "Saint Michael" because his caring made such a difference in her life at a most heartbreaking time.

With newfound confidence Marie studied and became a skilled counselor for troubled children. She told me a success story about passing on the gladness through being a caregiver, as Michael had been for her. She worked with a little "empty-faced" fourth-grader named Wayne, who couldn't read. He was a small child, impoverished in every way. Out of his mouth tumbled pure filth most of the time. Marie said: "When he called me a disgusting, profane name, I went into the rest room, put a daub of soap in my hand, returned to Wayne, and washed around his mouth, all the while explaining to him why I was doing this. Yes, I suppose I could have been fired. Yes, he hated me more than ever at that moment. But when school started in the fall, Wayne was back with me by choice, and our work on his literacy skills was a happy undertaking. Wayne knew I cared about what happened to him, and he finally hugged me in gladness when he had learned to sing the alphabet song straight through with no mistakes. One day Wayne's other teacher listened to him recite the alphabet and clapped when he finished successfully. Wayne looked over at me and said to her, 'Now we clap for Marie, because she taught me.' I was thrilled. I felt I had helped *save* someone," Marie concluded.

As a family we tried valiantly over a long period of time to help a beloved family member in the well-being of her spirit and, eventually, the preservation of her life. We cared for her in every way we could until the situation was beyond our influence. At her funeral her brother spoke in a remarkable voice of gladness that shifted our grief to a higher plane:

"As the end drew near for Christine, we all struggled with disappointment and hurt that the miracle had not come, that our prayers and these priesthood blessings had not been answered. We had different plans. And then, when our own hearts were broken, we began to recognize the hand of the Lord. We consciously tried to place Christine in God's hands. We acknowledged that we, the doctors and nurses, and even Christine herself had done all that we could do, and thus we tried to submit to His will.

"Finally, the answers began to come. We had prayed. All we wanted was for Christine to be safe, to be healed in body and spirit, to have a little peace and happiness at last, and to be able to continue to rear her children. And the Lord whispered to our hearts, 'She will be safe. She will be healed. Where else can she find peace and happiness? She has taught her children well, and they will still feel her love and guidance.' Do you see? Our prayers were answered. The miracle finally came. No, it wasn't what we *thought* we wanted. No, it wasn't what we had planned. But God in great mercy and goodness fulfilled his promises and gave us all what Christine *really* needed—rest, safety, healing, and joy.

"Some years ago Christine read an article by Dr. Carlfred Broderick that changed her life. Dr. Broderick described how some people become 'Saviors on Mount Zion.' The Church teaches that we do this by doing for others what they cannot do themselves. People will sacrifice greatly so that they may spare others suffering, or so that they may change the hearts of others. In so doing, such people become like the Savior. . . . We have imagined Christine in the premortal existence saying to the Lord, 'Yes, if that is how I can bless others, if that is how I can help them come unto thee, I am willing to do *even that.*'"

The following words of Frances Hall are dedicated to you who give care in a variety of important ways, however small they may seem. You can be doing some very simple thing, like serving meals, doing laundry for the sick, watering a plant, fluffing a pillow, or . . .

> You can be doing some very simple thing:
> Picking beans in a garden,
> Making sandwiches for a picnic,
> Helping a child put on his galoshes—
> And suddenly contentment splashes on your face
> Like a first drop of rain in an unexpected shower.
> A downpour of gentleness shines around you,
> There is an exuberant flash of lightning,
> And along the green hills of your life
> Resounds a thunderclap of joy.
>
> ("Special Moment," *Improvement Era,* October 1964, p. 845.)

7

The Flow'rs of Grace Appear

People are remarkable. Heavenly Father has such lovely children on earth in our day—perhaps in every day, if history can be believed. But the anonymous, low-key hosts who thoughtfully position themselves in such a way as to lift spirits, bring heaven closer in a frantic world, do kindness and generate goodness just by being there, are commendable. And there in their midst, and in memory as well, the flow'rs of grace appear, as the sunshine hymn suggests.

When President Ezra Taft Benson passed away, a grand, benevolent spirit descended upon the Salt Lake Valley. At least those connected with this revered leader and beloved prophet felt it so. By the time the thousands had lined up for the viewing, with little children being taught by conscientious parents what *it* all meant and who *he* was, by the time throngs everywhere had watched the funeral proceedings by satellite or participated in person in the buildings on Temple Square, peace and comfort and trust welled in every heart. Jesus was in charge and the flow'rs of grace had appeared along with breathtaking floral pieces for the funeral itself. Included here is a very special perspective of the hour following the funeral, when the cortege made its way to the Benson burial plot in Whitney, Idaho. It is a letter written by Pauline Edgley to the editor of the *Deseret*

News, and it points out what anonymous people can do to pass the sunshine, to minister with love—just by their presence, just by being there!

"As a person privileged to ride in President Benson's funeral cortege, in the car immediately ahead of the hearse, I want to share what was to me the most touching experience of the entire event.

"The entire distance from Salt Lake City to Whitney, Idaho, people were out in great numbers, lining the freeway, and on every overpass as far as Ogden, waiting and watching for the hearse bearing President Benson's body. . . . People waved, or stood at attention. Hats were removed, hands put over hearts, flags waved. In front of Woods Cross High School, possibly 100 large American flags had been erected along the fence, on which was placed a very large sign saying, 'President Benson, we love you! Woods Cross 2nd Ward,' and scores of people lined the fence to wave goodbye.

"That was just the beginning. People had brought their little children or had come as individuals. Some had obviously just stopped what they were doing to come watch for the cortege; others had planned well ahead. To pay their respects, many had dressed in their Sunday clothes that Saturday afternoon. On one overpass near Kaysville stood a whole group of fully uniformed Scouts, smartly saluting as we went by, behind a banner of love for our prophet. Driving along the freeway, frequently other cars recognized that they were driving alongside this cortege, and they pulled over to respectfully watch it pass.

"Nearing Logan, one house facing the highway had a sign covering the whole upper story proclaiming 'We thank thee O God for a Prophet' with 30 or more dressed up family members standing by the road waving as we went by. Stopping at a stoplight in Logan we noticed among the assembled crowd next to our car two little girls in Sunday clothes, holding up their copies of the Book of Mormon and little American flags.

"We . . . were impressed that so very many did come on their own, all along the way. It was a true grass-roots outpouring of love for our beloved prophet and brought tears to our eyes many times as we witnessed these scenes. A sincere thank you to each person who participated." ("Cortege's Path Marked with Love," *Deseret News,* 11 June 1994, p. A-9.)

Be glad if you are a caregiver! That is another name for "angel." When you are one who gives a care, Christ seems close and that's when his flow'rs of grace appear.

Never mind the beginnings of duty. Rather, think of what you have grown into—a kind of ministering angel—an instrument in the hands of God to bring sunshine and gladness to the sick and afflicted, the heartbroken, and the world-weary who can't pull out of the slump alone.

You'll find rewards in your work if you think about it this way. Not only are you a politician, a salesman, a fashion model, a computer whiz, or a media mogul by way of profession, but you dispense the inimitable goodness of making the best of a difficult situation. Your work is about well-being. For this brief moment forget the reasons that brought you to this demanding situation. Bask, instead, in the flood of love and gratitude people truly feel for those of you who help and help and help and help and . . .

Then the holy flow'rs of grace appear. Then the whole situation changes.

Sounds like real ministering angels to me!

When Amaleki turned the plates of sacred records over to King Benjamin, son of the beloved King Mosiah, he exhorted "all men to come unto God, the Holy One of Israel, and believe in prophesying, and in revelations, and in the *ministering of angels,* . . . and in all things which are good" (Omni 1:25, emphasis added). This reminds us that ministering angels are part of the blessings we may obtain as believers and receivers of the Holy Ghost. There are many instances of the ministering of angels in our religious literature: Knowing that John the Baptist had been imprisoned, Jesus sent angels to minister to him (see JST, Matthew 4:11). Joseph Smith, of course, was tutored by the angel Moroni.

When someone seems moved upon in a special way to

be of wonderful service to a person in deep need, we tend
to equate such a blessing with the ministering of angels. To
refer to a family member, friend, or other caregiver as, figuratively, a "ministering angel" is to pay that person a high
compliment, for angels are ministers of Christ, and they are
subject unto him to minister according to the word of his
command. It also gives us something more to think about
in relation to the Book of Mormon scripture that says that
angels have not ceased "to minister unto the children of
men" (Moroni 7:29). In the Doctrine and Covenants we
read: "Now, what do we hear in the gospel which we have
received? A voice of gladness! A voice of mercy from
heaven; and a voice of truth out of the earth; glad tidings
for the dead; a voice of gladness for the living and the
dead; glad tidings of great joy. How beautiful upon the
mountains are the feet of those that bring glad tidings of
good things." (D&C 128:19.)

The comparison of angels to nurses, selfless spouses,
patient mothers, visiting teachers, and therapists and aids
from the community center is not lightly made. Many
people have filled such a role in their own way, and what a
difference it has made in a tough situation! Because I've
been on the receiving end of such remarkable people, I
quickly add that whatever any such "angel" receives in return is not enough, with the possible exception of blessings
from heaven, which surely they enjoy as God's agents.

Richard's life, aside from a successful sales career, has
been totally geared to unobtrusively, faithfully, voluntarily
lightening the load and brightening the life of people with
problems. Now that he is retired he actually has a schedule
of people he visits, runs errands for, takes lunch and inspiring literature to, calls or visits to jog them along. In
Richard's earlier years there was his invalid brother for
whom he shouldered much of the care. People helped, of
course, but I have wondered if Richard has ever received
the sort of help he has given. This fine man is uncomfort-
able with fussing praise or thanks. He makes one believe he
would rather do basic kindness than anything else in life.
He is, nonetheless, loved and praised behind his humble,

helpful back, and he is remembered as Richard-Ray-of-Sunshine in prayers of gratitude.

In the scriptures and in the counsel given us by the Apostles in our day, we are promised that we do not have to struggle through life alone. My family can testify of that. We have been through the proverbial meat grinder in the last few years, yet at the same time we have been overwhelmed—even melted—by simple kindnesses and grand efforts at helping in a variety of problems that piled on us all at once like an earthquake's toll. We were told of being added to the temple prayer roll. The fresh pick of someone's flowers appeared at our home. A box of candy, a loaf of bread, a book were dropped by our door. Cards of encouragement and warm, hand-written messages changed the tone of a day. Sometimes just receiving word that our tears were blended with a friend's seemed a marvel. And we did not feel the burdens on our backs, thanks to the Lord Jesus Christ. Incredible, inimitable, and precious are such learnings and deepening of the soul.

We came to love people we hardly knew! Usually the ministering angels had been through a trial and refining of their own. For example, when Jim's paralyzed left side was joined by a broken hip on the right side, he was left an invalid. Though he would never fully recover, the adjustment process was assisted by choice caregivers who were trained spiritually as well as professionally. What is more, they believed as we believed! Their faith was like ours. Since we had little control over who was assigned to Jim's case, we felt that we were given special heavenly help in the matter. The paid caregivers became friends who ministered Christian service beyond the call of duty.

There was Rigamor Tuttle, an eighty-two-year-old widow who helped us in a time of need. Snow, sleet, rain, and clear—whatever the weather—she unfailingly came to us on the bus from where she lived at the south end of the valley to our home at the northern foothills. She inevitably brought sunshine into the sickroom. She came pert and pretty and in goodness. She was refined, humble, and helpful. This dear lady even refused gifts and refreshment in a stance of giving not taking. She came to relieve the major caregiver—me—and to give diversion to the patient. Mostly she just sat by Jim's bed and read to him. As Jim healed, she would read from books she had never heard of before. She read periodicals and tomes of particular interest to my history-buff spouse. Rigamor claimed it was an education for her and often went to the library to study up on something they had talked about. Incredible! We were glad that Sister Tuttle had been a Gospel Doctrine teacher, because she would read the weekly assignment to him as well as other scriptural selections which he longed to hear.

One day while Rigamor was with us a great promise of the Lord recounted in the Book of Mormon flooded my heart. I *knew* that she was an answer to prayer for us. That day I asked her to begin her reading time with Jim from Mosiah 24. We wanted her to understand how grateful we were for *her* as well as for her assistance in being an instrument in the hand of God for the well-being of our troubled home. In this passage the Lord promises blessings to the people of Alma and assures them that he has heard their prayers and remembered the covenants they have made. He says, in verse 14, "And I will also ease the burdens which are put upon your shoulders, that even you cannot feel them upon your backs, even while you are in bondage."

Through Rigamor the Lord's promises were kept for us. Rigamor was a kind of ministering angel. She came with the healing Holy Spirit about her. She was practical, positive, and peaceful. Her help was from her prayerful heart. One can give gratitude for "a Rigamor" only by thanking God and finding ways to pass on the sunshine in serving others.

Now, caregivers don't just deal with sickness. Caregivers show up among Heavenly Father's children on earth all along the paths of life. A schoolteacher stood in our testimony meeting and told about accepting a call to substitute in a Primary class of nine-year-olds. She is a teacher all week by profession. She is a busy mother of a growing family. She has her own Church calling and did not *need* to substitute teach a bunch of "destroying, disrupting angels"

noted for their unruliness in Primary. She said that what
made matters worse was that the subject was "fasting and
prayer." She was certain they'd be bored and wild. But
Kitty is a true believer, a humble helper where needed. She
decided to fast and pray about this assignment. She fervently asked Heavenly Father not only to bless her but also
to pour out his Spirit upon the children that they might be
still and listen. Much to the comfort of the parents of these
nine-year-olds, Kitty witnessed in that fast and testimony
meeting that her prayers were answered—the children all
listened! Later, one of the parents reported that his child
had talked about that lesson all during family dinner, something that hadn't happened a lot at their house!

We have a colorful friend so gifted that she might be
threatening to one less fortunate in life's advantages. Her
family was living away from their extended family and from
a full bursting Church program when their only daughter
had to undergo a kidney transplant. The people in their
Little Rock neighborhood called Karen "the miracle girl."
They were people of many different races and religions, but
together they fasted and prayed and did household kindnesses and "taxi duty" to ease the burden upon this young
family. They weren't all members of the local Relief Society,
whose help in such times is almost expected. They were
neighbors who may or may not be part of a congregation of
worship. Later, they jokingly formed the Caregivers
Corporation for the "business" of freely easing the pain of
people in trouble. They had never had such a spiritual experience before, you see, and they were anxious to try it
again because of the meaning and worth it gave to life.

The last part of the verse from Mosiah applies here:
"And this will I do that ye may stand as witnesses for me
hereafter, and that ye may know of a surety that I, the Lord
God, do visit my people in their afflictions" (24:14).

Those who need care and those who give it always
trade places sooner or later. Life lets us see both sides of
the coin. Those who give care and those who receive it
surely smooth the whole process by remembering a favorite childhood song: "Jesus wants me for a sunbeam, to

shine for him each day; in ev'ry way try to please him. . . ." (Nellie Talbot, "Jesus Wants Me for a Sunbeam," *Children's Songbook,* p. 60.) Realists often don't include this perky song these days, but it is a tool of gladness and joy just the same. These stories of caregivers are shared, not to praise or glorify them inappropriately, but to prove the incredible difference that can be made in a life, in a personality, in a set of circumstances by a caregiver willing to invest "self under inspiration."

People who knew Dr. Keith Engar recall his rare contribution to the Church and to the university community. He was the general chairman of the Church Activities Committee until shortly before his illness struck. Keith always wanted to do what was honorable. During the last days of his ill health and mental confusion, his caregiver and darling wife Amy (one and the same!) discovered how deep this inclination really went. Keith had memorized the Scout Oath in his youth, and he deliberately repeated it each day during his last great struggle. Finally, he couldn't recite the oath, but he still formed the accompanying sign. Performing this ritual was a final stirring act before he went on to heaven! It was all he could muster, but it sent a message of spiritual strength and reassurance to his Amy. Afterward, Amy admitted that her long season of privileged caregiving was summed up by that last valiant gesture of a man of honor. It was a rich reward for her. What a man . . . and what a woman!

Caregivers often need to simply make the most of what there is. When her ex-husband was in the last stages of AIDS, Evalyn brought him to her condo so that she could take care of him, minister to his needs, and make life as pleasant as possible. She made the most of what there was. She played his favorite classics on the CD player. She read from the books he loved. She presented his food to him with fresh flowers or a note of encouragement. She arranged for conference calls, handled his business records, and invested in a speaker phone so he could visit with the people he cared for without having to be seen. Their affection for each other was rekindled with new overtones. His last words to her were, "Evalyn, you have overwhelmed me with gladness that I know you." Compassion revisited!

People who pass on the sunshine to someone who is in a dark season of life often have one hand on the patient but the other one in God's. Keeping very close to the Spirit while serving as a caregiver can enhance the task, giving it the enduring edge of spirituality. You may serve in a way you won't understand until a later time.

You may be part of a miracle, as young Dr. Richardson was. He was an exhausted anesthesiologist going off duty, when a doctor friend asked him to fill in for a cesarean section because his own brother had suffered a massive heart attack. Dr. Richardson knew nothing of the case but agreed to help out. Twins were coming and there were complications. Dr. Richardson prayed for strength and guidance. It is up to the anesthesiologist to revive or awaken the patient. This patient did not respond. Dr. Richardson mentally searched his training for the right procedures to follow to bring her back to life. He did what he could, but when he finally left the scene she was in a deep coma. Details too sacred and private to reveal here proved the young doctor's skill and spirit as a caregiver. The next day the woman revived completely and asked to meet the young doctor who had attended her as the anesthesiologist. She told him of seeing people dressed in white in a prayer circle behind him, yearning for him and his success in this difficult situation. The woman's future depended on him—including the privilege of rearing the new twins. Later she came to his home and studied family pictures until she found people she recognized as having been in the prayer circle. She was so grateful for Dr. Richardson's prayerful care! She recognized proof of his value to the work of the Lord on earth because she had witnessed the concern *for him* of those who had already gone beyond the veil and because she had learned something about her own mission that impacted her choice to come back to life. What he did made returning to life a medical possibility. Caregivers may not perceive the importance of what they are doing.

Caregivers function at every level.

I have spent a great deal of time in medical clinics and hospitals, and I never cease to marvel at the caregivers among us. Wives hobbling along beside sturdy husbands. Husbands being wheeled, shaved, and dressed by wives. Children being carried into the clinic by fathers who manage to get time off work to do these heavies. Doctors, nurses, and technicians gently moving people into heartbreak territory as frightening truth is uncovered.

We have precedents in history—plenty of trouble always abroad in the land. But one thing to remember in our day is that for the most part caregivers sleep between clean sheets, after a full meal and a slick flush of the facilities. We don't suffer in a brutal civil massacre. We don't birth our babies, only to bury them and then pick up our wagons and head west. We are not innocent victims of a holocaust, a racial cleansing, or medical experimentation. We are no longer constantly threatened with mob violence. We have not endured inquisition or slavery. From magnificent people who have suffered, we have learned mighty lessons of accommodation, of enduring and even flourishing, of cultivating a wholesome attitude of cheerful, patient submission before the Lord's will. And not only will it turn out all right, but we can pass on the gladness as we go!

As the Psalmist counseled, "Serve the Lord with gladness: come before his presence with singing" (Psalm 100:2). Of course, we are in his presence when we give service "unto one of the least of these," because then we are serving him. How pleasant to think of going before him and serving happily, serving with a smile and a song, dispensing our caregiving with sunshine until the flow'rs of his grace appear.

We are reminded in Ecclesiastes that there is a time to be born and a time to die. Seldom noticed in the context of this lovely, poetic truth is a telling line about life: "[God] hath set the world in their heart, so that no man can find out the work that God maketh from the beginning to the end" (Ecclesiastes 3:11). We only know that we *must* go through the paces of this journey from earth to heaven. It helps when there are helpers—givers of gladness and people who pass on the sunshine in a variety of ways. Choice and circumstance impact one's life. So do caregivers. They are even able to point out the silver lining in the current dark cloud, not to mention the "joys laid up above" for the stricken. And when caregivers are the stricken it is often because the trials of caring for others go on for so long. But surely, as they serve, they too are laying up God's joys.

Now, aren't you glad you are a caregiving, ministering angel, along with a whole host of sunshine-sharing others?

Stephen Levin wrote: "If you were going to die soon and had only one phone call you could make, who would you call and what would you say? And why are you waiting?"

8

Fathers and Sunshine

"I'm glad you are my dad! What if I didn't have such a great dad?" Cameron said as he positioned the identification tag under the seat of his new bike. The tag read: "Cameron Daley, 2121 Beaverlake Drive, age 7."

Cameron felt his father's big hand steady his smaller one as the tag was secured. At last, his own bike! And the ID tag proved it. "Dad, I really like my new bike, and hey, you are some kind of awesome." Then Cameron reached to give his dad's arm a squeeze.

Cameron's father smiled. "Good! Now, your bike has your name on it, just as you have my name on you."

"Yeah," responded Cameron absentmindedly as he smoothed his hand over the handlebar.

"Listen, son, take care of you *and* your bike, will you? Believe me, you and your bike had better not show up someplace where you have no business being!"

"Right." Cameron slipped his foot onto the pedal and adjusted his helmet.

"Did you hear me? And keep that helmet on, okay?"

"Okay. Okay! Sure, Dad, I'll keep my helmet on if you will keep your cool. Okay?" Cameron loved his dad, but he wanted to get on with life and bike riding.

"Okay, but remember about the whole armour of God that we talked about last night. Got it?"

"Got it!" answered Cameron, already wheeling off with a "grin full of sunshine," as Mom always said. And Dad mumbled to himself, "Proverbs 10:1: 'A wise son maketh a glad father.' "

Almost everybody is glad for you, Dad, whether you think you are awesome or not. It is your caring and your yearning after them—bailing those offspring out of trouble and shifting them into happier ways—that really make a difference in a person's life. You are good for much more than that, too. For example, as a worthy priesthood holder you have the right to preside at special moments involving the laying on of hands—a name and a blessing; the healing blessing; baptism and confirmation; a special blessing before school starts, when assignments loom, or as a mission or marriage get under way. Such blessings can bring comfort and can inspire trust.

How about the aching times on your knees and the sleepless nights when "that boy" defies you as he tries to be a man (like you, Dad)? There may be open battling, yes, but what about the good times when your strong arm, your warm arm of safety, your kind of affection, your reassuring praise work wonders?

Your love isn't passive, though it may not be demonstrative. Some fathers are famous for playing it aloof, but that isn't true of *all* fathers! There are many ways of taking fatherly responsibility and showing love. There is only one sure way to bring a son into the light of the Lord, and that is by example.

There was a teacher who counted fathers' influence as most important in today's world of dysfunctional families and permissive attitudes. She decided to try and get their attention by telling them that on such and such a night their children would be sharing their essays on the theme "What I Like About My Dad."

The men came, of course. They came in their small sports cars, their campers, their super-trucks, and their compacts. They came in clothing reflecting their daily work, their lifestyle, their personal taste. They came with certain apprehension, as well. And interesting to note, most of them came without a spouse. The thinking seemed to be that they didn't want ammunition made available for the wife to use, in case the essays were less than glowing!

The essays turned out to be a lot alike. The children talked about a special thing that Dad *did*—something that meant Dad was a friend. Nobody mentioned how much money he had, what kind of car he drove, what clothes he wore, how he looked, the size of house he provided, or what he did for work.

Each father came to that meeting with his own view of his fathering. Each left with a conviction that companionship with the child was what counted.

In these latter days great fathers have trained up great sons, and both have contributed to the kingdom of God on earth in remarkable ways. George F. Richards and his son LeGrand Richards were both Apostles. Joseph F. Smith and his son Joseph Fielding Smith were prophets and Presidents of the Church. Brigham Young was prophet and President of the Church, and his son Brigham Young Jr. was an Apostle. The same was true of Wilford Woodruff and his son Abraham Owen Woodruff.

Because of their relationship, I specifically include here my husband's grandfather George Q. Cannon, who served as an Apostle and as a Counselor in the First Presidency, and his son (my husband's father) Sylvester Q. Cannon, who was also an Apostle.

As a family we treasure the wisdom and insight that we found in the private papers of Sylvester Cannon. He was an engineer by profession and a gentle, refined man of God through parental training. Before his mission as a young man, Sylvester traveled with his father, serving as his "secretary" on several trips. That experience provided a sure polishing for him through daily companionship with his father, which included frequent daily prayer, preaching and teaching, blessing the Saints, and sharing the gospel with nonmembers. Sylvester grew up to become the father of seven loyal children and to serve as a mission president, stake president, and Presiding Bishop of the Church for thirteen years. He was ordained an Apostle in 1938, and he served as an Associate to the Quorum of the Twelve until becoming a member of that body in 1939. His youngest son, my husband, D.J. Cannon, was reared and trained in righteousness and reverence for his forefathers who served the Lord valiantly. To his own posterity, Jim has passed along his own clear wisdom for life and devotion to gospel principles. For example, this quote from Grandfather George Q. Cannon has helped our family over many hurdles: "Though your prayers may not be answered immediately, if they are offered in the name of Jesus and in faith, nothing being left undone by you that is required, they will live on the records of Heaven and in the remembrance of the Lord and yet bear fruit."

With such fathers as we have talked about here, there is a legacy that is most precious and remarkable, really, that can pass from father to son and prove the cultural and spiritual salvation of the generations.

Lynn Bennion has been one of the great educators of our time. His humanitarian style was to give all men their chance in the system. He clearly remembers his inner feelings when he was a young man and his father said a few words that changed his thinking forever.

World War I saw America and Germany as enemies, and the carryover of feelings was difficult to change. An immigrant family from Germany moved into the farm community that was the Bennion family's neighborhood. They were the Buehners and they were good, hard-working people, but language was a problem and so they were not readily assimilated into the social structure. This was not a stigma against this particular German family per se. Rather it was a blight of the times against all people from the Old Country. Dr. Bennion remembers well the Sunday morning when his benevolent father put his arm around Lynn and spoke gently but firmly to him and his younger brother, "My sons, go and sit by the Buehner boys in Sunday School. They're lonesome." They did as their father told them. And the Buehner boys and the Bennion boys grew up to be prosperous and serving and to be significant leaders among men.

Carl Buehner served as a General Authority of the Church. It was my privilege to be part of his group of Church leaders on a leadership training tour in Europe. In each of the Church areas in Germany, Elder Buehner told a dramatic story of what he had learned from his father. Now a successful American businessman and an important Church leader, Carl Buehner stood before the people of his birth land to describe his first real job in America. It was hard manual labor. Each day he had to haul huge sacks of cement, loading and unloading them to fill orders and re-plenish storage bins. Each sack of cement was stamped with the company's name and logo—a huge red devil complete with horns and pitchfork! Brother Buehner said his father taught him that when you wrestled with the devil in life it was hard work to get free of the burden. Carl Buehner grew to hate the devil. "With each bag of cement I lifted and toted I'd remember the lesson, and I vowed not to mess with the real devil!" Carl said.

A rare insight into the impact of a father upon his son for good comes from Julian Dyke, who writes: "When I was young, our little family lived in a one-bedroom apartment on the second floor. I slept on the couch in the living room. . . . My dad, a steelworker, left home very early for work each day. Every morning he would quietly close the windows I had opened in the living room; then he would tuck the covers around me and stop for a minute. I would be half-dreaming when I could sense my dad standing be-side the couch, looking at me. As I slowly awoke, I became embarrassed to have him there. I tried to pretend I was still asleep, but his gaze made me squirm. I became aware that as he stood beside my bed he was praying with all his at-tention, energy, and focus—for me.

"Each morning my dad prayed for me. He prayed that I would have a good day, that I would be safe, that I would learn and prepare for the future. And since he could not be with me until evening, he prayed for the teachers and my friends that I would be with that day.

"In junior high and high school, I reached my dream to be an athlete. . . . Our football games were usually played on Friday evenings. My father now worked out of town for a defense contractor during the week. But each Friday afternoon, he left work and drove six or seven hours to make it to every one of my games. He never arrived in time for the start of the game, but the coaches would leave a sideline pass at the gate for him. I knew that sometime during the first half, I would look up and there he would be on the sideline, watching me. Then after church on Sunday afternoons, he would have to turn around and drive back to work.

"At first, I didn't really understand what my dad was doing those mornings when he prayed for me. But as I got older, I came to sense his love and interest in me and everything I was doing. It is one of my favorite memories." ("Thanks, Dad," *New Era*, April 1993, p. 38.)

Vaughn Featherstone's sons learned about honoring the priesthood from their dad as he took care to dress in a jacket and tie to perform the comforting priesthood ordinance of a healing blessing for one of them.

Burke Peterson's story of learning from his father about giving his best to the Church is a notable one. He remembers a wonder-filled feeling as he saw his father ironing the paper dollars of the tithes and offerings before he turned them over to a higher authority. He wanted everything to be as neat and orderly and cared for as possible!

One of the abiding blessings of my own life is remembering the way I felt every time I saw my father "crinkle his eyes with tears," as we children called it, when one of us gave some little verse in grade school umpteen years ago or gave a talk in the Tabernacle later on. Unapologetically, he did this same tender thing as he introduced us to his business friends or to his work staff when we, in Halloween dress-ups, dropped in at his office. The measure of security, well-being, and gladness that a father's evident love can mean to a child is inestimable.

Doug Bagley is a man loved for a lot of reasons. At least one of them is evident in the context of his being a father with a demanding career, one that involves professionally helping others. When we were with him for several hours taking care of necessary work in his storage area and warehouse, we noticed the relationship between Doug and his six-year-old son, John. This bright-eyed boy followed his dad around in keen interest, not with sulky impatience nor whining demands. This boy knew what his father's work was! He was learning it. He learned about interacting with customers, some of them under much stress, as he was introduced to them. He used the speaker system to send messages. He ran errands and followed the instructions his father gave, almost as a matter of course. Clearly this young boy had been at work before. John learned to "work" in ways that stretched the mind, muscles, and scope of the lad. He watched and learned as one who was a part of it all, not a spectator. John noted the occasional pat, squeeze, and soda pop from his father. I noted the hero worship in the boy's look. He liked being with his dad in the workplace.

I watched the boy watch the father's warm greeting of the mother when she arrived. Then came the crowning moment for me. As John and his father accompanied me to the door the boy, looking back to his dad, explained, "He is my *one* father! I am sealed to him. I am *sealed to him*. Mother is my only and always mother." He wasn't just imparting information to me, his newfound friend, rather it was an announcement of the lucky situation he gladly found himself in.

I mean to say, for what more could a child ask?

Smith Shumway is a remarkable man who lost his sight during World War II. He had been well into medical school, training for a career that demanded sharp eyes, among other things. That war injury changed his life forever, but a remarkable attitude and great faith were his help. Now, for over forty years, Smith has worked miracles with people who have lost their sight. He is quick to credit his father for his inspiring recovery and exemplary attitude of faith. "[My parents] taught me to pray for light and to desire knowledge," he said.

A relative had criticized him with the observation that if Smith had prayed as *her* son had, who was alive and well

75

in a German prison camp, he might not have lost his sight. Smith took the rebuff kindly, remembering that he had prayed and that he was in good company with the outcome—hadn't Jesus himself prayed that the cup would pass from him? For Smith, as for Jesus and a whole parade of faithful fathers and sons through the ages, the attitude of happiness and peace remains: "Not my will, but thine, be done" (Luke 22:42).

It is as the ancient philosopher said (and many have quoted since), "Like father, like son," and as Jesus taught, "Every good tree bringeth forth good fruit." There it is again—that sacred connection between Jesus and sunshine, Dad and sons' shine.

9

When the Lord Is Near

How beautifully the poet sets the stage for considerations on the benefits of being in the Lord's light: springtime—inimitable springtime—fills the soul because the Lord is near. With such lines, it is no wonder that the old hymn "There is Sunshine in My Soul Today" is still beloved among the Saints.

The sunflower is a symbol of God's light and creation. Sundials in old-fashioned gardens or new-sculptured grounds frequently are engraved with these lines: "Light-enchanted Sunflower, thou who gazest ever true and tender on the sun's revolving splendour!" Is it expanding the point to suggest that there are certain people in certain times who stand head and shoulders above the crowd, who ever reach "true and tender" for the sun—the light—to bask in enlightenment.

There is the perspective that some people are heroes and go about lighting lamps for the rest of us to see by; but a saint is himself a light. Wasn't the Prophet Joseph Smith such a person?

How glad we are that fourteen-year-old Joseph sought the light of the heavens for guidance about church membership and worship. God was waiting, listening, and he chose to answer the boy Joseph's prayer with a wonderful vision in which the Gods themselves appeared—for Joseph saw God the Father, who introduced His Beloved Son. Now the world could know the true nature of God and his plan for mankind. We praise "the man who communed with Jehovah" so that full joy could become available to us.

President S. Dilworth Young wrote a poetic saga in tribute to Joseph Smith. It is called *The Long Road* and is about various events and aspects of the Prophet's life. As an editor of Church magazines, I was sitting in President Young's office discussing an article he was preparing. He asked me to stay and listen to something else he had written. It was the tribute in verse to the Prophet Joseph— to the singular contribution he made to the fulness of light in our lives and to the work of the restoration of the gospel among men. I recall sitting very still then and suddenly feeling surprised at how deeply involved I became in the work, how alive and believable the Prophet Joseph became in those moments. Of course, I loved this work and urged him to finish it for publication. It was a privilege to observe the workings of the mind of this creative thinker. We talked over certain passages, and it was a treasured time for me. To further encourage publication of the work, we enter- tained in our home a large number of friends and fans of Dilworth Young. His gentle, lyrical, sensible reading of *The Long road* was impressive. It was a happy spring evening just after daylight saving time began to lengthen our evenings. He stood in the aura of natural light of the sunset streaming behind him through large open doors. The group was enthusiastic about the work and its proposed publica- tion. *The Long Road* was indeed published, and it was cir- culated far and wide.

The following lines are about the birth and miracle naming of Joseph:

> What shall we name him?
> This question,
> Part of every birth,
> Common as the stones which
> Build the hearth,

Must be squarely met.
For names most truly
Set the tone,
The fibre of the living soul.
The father speaks:
I feel, he says,
To name him after me.
The mother's echoing words
Find favor with her man.
He shall, says she,
Be named after his father's name;
So shall his name be
Joseph!

(From *The Long Road* [Salt Lake City: Book-craft, 1967], p. 11.)

This choice of name fulfills ancient prophecy. For example, old father Lehi had been teaching his sons and giving each a father's blessing. To his last-born son he said: "Joseph, . . . thy seed shall not utterly be destroyed. For behold, thou art the fruit of my loins; and I am a descendant of Joseph who was carried captive into Egypt. . . . [That] Joseph truly saw our day. . . . Yea, Joseph truly said: Thus saith the Lord unto me: A choice seer will I raise up out of the fruit of thy loins. . . . And his name shall be called after me; and it shall be after the name of his father. And he shall be like unto me; for the thing, which the Lord shall bring forth by his hand, by the power of the Lord shall bring my people unto salvation." (2 Nephi 3:3–5, 7, 15.)

Imagine: his name was known back then! The scriptural account continues: "And there shall rise up one mighty among them, who shall do much good, both in word and in deed, being an instrument in the hands of God, with exceeding faith, to work mighty wonders, and do that thing which is great in the sight of God, unto the bringing to pass much restoration unto the house of Israel, and unto the seed of thy brethren" (2 Nephi 3:24).

What a prophet!

What a grand instrument he was!

He disciplined himself. He reached out to people. He paid a price in personal preparation and in personal choice to be what he became. He sacrificed all along the way. He brought about the establishment of the Church and laid the groundwork for the incredible system of instruction, opportunity, ordinances, and blessings which enriches us today. We can only express the smallest part of the happiness we feel about what Joseph did in the name of the Lord. Perhaps there will come a day when we will be able to gladly express gratitude to Joseph Smith himself!

Following the dedication service of the Oakland Temple, there was a sweet, warm sociality among those of us who were in the foyer. People had come from far places to be part of this highly spiritual occasion. We were with another couple from Salt Lake. The two men and I had held general Church positions that gave us the opportunity to travel widely for the Church. The other woman had not traveled as we had. The three of us hugged old friends and visited with people from scattered states. The other woman stood, pressed back against a wall in the foyer, waiting patiently for us.

As we walked to the car, my friend hooked her arm through mine and said thoughtfully, "You know, that was a heavenly experience; but sadly, I have never felt so out of place in all my life, because I didn't know anybody. I have decided to go back home and learn something about the people who are important to me who are already in heaven. Someday I want to be where they are, and when I get there I want to know something about them and have something to talk to them about." She mentioned Jesus, Joseph Smith, her great-grandparents who had accepted the gospel and migrated to Salt Lake. That was November. By February she had passed away. It was a dramatic lesson for me.

In my studies since then, particularly into the life of Joseph Smith, I have been blessed to receive a testimony that Joseph Smith did see both the Father and the Son and that he was tutored by heavenly beings. The "angel story," as some scoffers describe Joseph's sacred vision, should not be difficult to accept. In fact, it would be disappointing in the extreme if God were *not* to deal with his children in this supernatural manner when the occasion requires it. It puts a limit on God to think that he could not manifest himself under such circumstances.

Like many of you, I am glad that I have taken the treks through Church history country. I have slept on the site of Joseph's birth in Sharon, Vermont. I have felt the protective spirit there. I have gazed in silent thanksgiving at the tall monument to him. It is a granite shaft—one huge stone 38½ feet high, one foot for each year of the Prophet's life. I have scrambled under brush to look at the original foundation of the Joseph Smith Sr. home. I have fingered the gnarled orchard trees, remnants of those childhood days of the boy Joseph a century and a half ago. There was a time when I was there when the snow was hip high, as it must have been on 23 December 1805, when Joseph was born. And walking that path, the picture came clearly to my mind of the events happening in the little cabin during such a season.

I have walked the long road in Palmyra to the Sacred Grove—I've prayed and preached there too. I have sung "A Poor Wayfaring Man of Grief" and been duly sobered at the bloodstains in Carthage Jail. I've grieved at Liberty Jail and found new value in D&C 121. All this to become better acquainted with the Prophet and founder of The Church of Jesus Christ of Latter-day Saints who is so dear to my family.

Having known the Prophet personally, Grandfather George Q. Cannon wrote a book about him titled *Life of Joseph Smith the Prophet.* In that book, Grandfather Cannon wrote about the first time he ever saw Joseph Smith: "The occasion was the arrival of a large company of Latter-day Saints at the upper landing at Nauvoo. The general conference of the Church was in session and large numbers crowded to the landing place to welcome the emigrants. Nearly every prominent man in the community was there. Familiar with the names of all and the persons of many of the prominent elders, the author sought with a boy's curiosity and eagerness, to discover those whom he knew, and especially to get sight of the Prophet and his brother Hyrum, neither of whom he had ever met. When his eyes fell upon the Prophet, without a word from anyone to point him out, or any reason to separate him from others who stood around, he knew him instantly. He would have known him among ten thousand. There was that about him, which to the author's eyes, distinguished him from all the men he had ever seen." (*Life of Joseph Smith the Prophet* [1888; reprint, Salt Lake City: Deseret Book Co., 1986], pp. 20–21.)

Years later George Q. Cannon stated in a discourse: "The Saints could not comprehend Joseph Smith; the Elders could not; the Apostles could not. They did so a little toward the close of his life; but his knowledge was so extensive and his comprehension so great that they could not rise to it." (*Millennial Star* 61 [5 October 1899]: 629.)

When I was an editor of the youth magazine of the Church, we published impressions that youth in the Prophet's day had of him (see Truman G. Madsen, "Portrait of a Prophet," Era of Youth section, *Improvement Era,* December 1963, pp. 1138–50). You see, one of the main benefits of studying the life and contribution of a great leader is that there are lessons to be learned from his example. Much of what follows comes from the magazine article:

A thirteen-year-old lad, small for his age, watched the Prophet during the Zion's Camp march. He idealized Joseph's strength and said he was "a tall, well-built man." A girl who at sixteen left her home and came to Nauvoo said: "His majesty of appearance was something wonderful. You would think he was much taller and much larger even than he was." Later she wrote that "there are no pictures of him extant that I know of that compare with the majesty of his presence." A convert from the Quaker movement observed that Joseph was not as "sedate and serious" as his brother Hyrum, and noted that he was "always so neat." An English boy, impressed with British royalty, observed that "he wore no whiskers" and that "altogether he presented a very formidable appearance being a man of gentlemanly bearing."

Others described him as less formal, outdoorsy, dressed in work clothes or in coats with thin elbows that proved he was a laborer. As a young man, Joseph B. Nobles learned about the gospel while haying alongside Joseph.

Wandle Mace wrote about how, as a young man in Illinois, he would visit the Prophet's parents and listen to Mother Smith tell of the stories Joseph used to tell the family about the early inhabitants of this continent—their clothing, mode of warfare, and lifestyle. Brother Mace also recorded that Joseph's love for sacred music was unmatched and that he wept when a small congregation sang, "Glorious Things Are Sung of Zion."

Sixteen-year-old Samuel Miles recognized Joseph's "easy, jovial appearance when engaged in sports" but also his "firm dislike of that which was degrading." Seventeen-year-old William Taylor spent two weeks with him while in hiding. "I have never felt the same joy and satisfaction in the companionship of any other person," he wrote.

John L. Smith was fifteen when he made a forced march with a segment of the Nauvoo Legion to protect Nauvoo. He looked up from a log where his feet left blood marks to see the Prophet in tears. "God bless you, God bless you, my dear boy," the Prophet said. "The sensation and impression can never be forgotten," wrote John.

Jedediah Grant, who delivered many missionary sermons before he was eighteen, said, "He [Joseph] could take the wisest of the Elders and circumscribe his very thoughts." Edward Stevenson, fourteen at the time he attended his first Church meeting, wrote, "I began to believe he possessed an infinity of knowledge."

The conferral of divine authority was so near and real to the Prophet that it was breathtaking to young men who came under his hands. One wrote that Joseph Smith "seemed to be just as familiar with the Spirit World and as well acquainted with the other side as he was here."

In the *Ensign* of January 1984 there was an excellent pictorial feature on the Prophet with a description of the now-famous meeting of Joseph Smith and Wilford Woodruff. Brother Woodruff wrote: "Before I saw Joseph I did not care how old he was, or how young he was. I did not care how he looked—whether his hair was long or short; the man that advanced that revelation was a prophet of God. I knew it for myself. I first met Joseph Smith in the streets of Kirtland. He had on an old hat, and a pistol in his hand. Said he, 'Brother Woodruff, I've been out shooting at a mark, and I wanted to see if I could hit anything.' And, said he, 'have you any objection to it?'

" 'Not at all,' said I. 'There is no law against a man shooting at a mark, that I know of.'

"He invited me to his house. He had a wolf skin, which he wanted me to help him to tan; he wanted it to sit on while driving his wagon team. Now, many might have said, 'You are a pretty prophet; shooting a pistol and tanning a wolf skin.' Well, he tanned it, and used it while making a journey of a thousand miles. This was my first acquaintance with the Prophet Joseph. And from that day until the present, with all the apostasies we have had, and with all the difficulties and afflictions we have been called to pass through, I never saw a moment when I had any doubt with regard to this work. I have had no trial about this. While the people were apostatizing on the right hand and on the left . . . it was no temptation to me to doubt this work or to doubt that Joseph Smith was a prophet of God." (As quoted in Buddy Youngreen, "From the Prophet's Life," p. 32.)

We owe an incredible debt of gratitude to Wilford Woodruff for a detailed record of the teachings and preaching of the Prophet Joseph Smith. I have seen in Wilford Woodruff's handwriting in his personal journal, which is in the Church archives, the statement that he could not go to sleep at night until he had recorded all that the Prophet Joseph had said. Brother Woodruff had total re-call, through the power of the Holy Ghost, he said, until the sermon was recorded, and then he would forget it.

On occasion, Brother Woodruff called certain others to record things in his private journal for him, depending on circumstance, perhaps. My own great-great-grandfather,

Major Howard Egan, wrote in Wilford Woodruff's personal records. Such records as well as the recollections of early Church members provide fascinating details about Joseph Smith. Bathsheba W. Smith recalled, for instance, that the Prophet gave the opening prayer at the sixth meeting of the Relief Society on 28 April 1842, a fact not recorded in the sisters' minutes of that meeting. She remembered that Brother Joseph's voice trembled greatly as he gave the prayer and that during the meeting he mentioned that he wouldn't be with them long. (See "Recollections of the Prophet Joseph Smith," *Juvenile Instructor* 27 [1 June 1892]: 345.)

The way the Prophet was, the way people felt in his presence, has carried over into our day. Surely we all understand what made him bigger than life, nearer to heaven than to earth, lively at his games and giving, but prophetic in his leadership. His was a power that came from heaven, of course, but he kept the faith, kept his own control, and was a splendid example for us.

I have held in my hand and read with my own eyes the original personal journal of Joseph Smith. It is locked in the Church vaults along with precious treasures of the kingdom, such as portions of the original manuscript of the translation of the Book of Mormon and the papyrus from which parts of the book of Abraham were translated. It was thrilling to me to turn the pages of that intimate little journal, written candidly by the Prophet Joseph Smith. At the top of the first page, his name and a partial sentence were written, then scratched out before he started over. The opening lines read:

"Joseph Smith Jrs Book for Record baught on the 27th of November 1832 for the purpose to keep a minute acount of all things that come under my obse[r]vation &c—

"Oh may God grant that I may be directed in all my thaughts Oh bless thy Servent Amen."

Joseph Smith had received a revelation that day which we know as section 85 of the Doctrine and Covenants. The revelation declared that the Lord had appointed a clerk "to keep a history, and a general church record of all things that transpire in Zion . . . ; and also their manner of life, their faith, and works" (D&C 85:1–2). Joseph, on the very day he received the revelation, bought a book for his own personal record of observation. What light and instruction this experience of reading Joseph's journal brought to me as a record keeper. I felt the Lord very near in those moments.

It is interesting to consider how a man of Joseph's confident nature and incredible, unique experiences and preparations by God would handle the division of authority when the organization of the First Presidency was directed by God. This event proves Joseph's obedience and unselfishness. He called two Counselors in March 1832, and so the First Presidency was organized. When the events at Carthage took place later, the Lord had already provided an authority structure to hold the gifts and carry the responsibility of the work of the kingdom at that time.

Joseph's life work began with obedience, and so, it seems, should ours. When confronted with a problem, he sought the solution by seeking light through counsel with God, who created us and appointed the principles by which we can live successfully. In the Bible Joseph read James 1:5: "If any of you lack wisdom, let him ask of God, that giveth to all men liberally, and upbraideth not; and it shall be given him." He followed this counsel. Because of that, we have the brilliant Church structure and scriptures and all that this means!

Read again the precious extracts from the history of Joseph Smith that are contained in the Pearl of Great Price. When my mother was old and ill I enjoyed reading the scriptures to her. On one occasion I was reading from Joseph's account of his visions. When I paused in the reading, assuming that she had fallen asleep, she immediately filled in the blanks. She *knew* that story! And when we finished she opened her eyes and said, "The important thing is that Joseph lived near to the Lord and was obedient."

I agree, for out of that obedience has come all the gladness we could know.

10

When Jesus Shows His Smiling Face

There was a pleasant little shop in a Rocky Mountain resort village full of an assortment of pleasant little shops featuring the creative collections and artistic efforts of some of God's most talented children of all ages. This particular pleasant little shop was named "Pleasant Things." The bay window display obviously was designed to conjure memories for the passersby and to entice them into buying back their happy past. Perhaps it was even meant to make a statement about present lifestyle.

There were wreaths of grape twigs, bunches of dried herbs and field flowers, and a wide variety of trendy bird-houses accessorized with a Spanish moss nest and small hummingbird eggs tucked next to the mammoth one of an ostrich. There were treasure boxes of all sizes, shapes, coverings, and quality, photo albums of cut velvet with antique hinges and clasps, embossed leather folders so lovely they seemed suitable only for the memoirs of very distinguished patriarchs, and strands of beads of such color and prism that a lady would need no other enhancement. There were miniature violet vases, clocks, bedsteads, wooden people nestled among silk scarves and ties, cake stands and jelly jars, weaving spool candlesticks, fading photographs with museum-quality frames. There were dolls of exquisite porcelain and Victorian finery next to whom Ken and Barbie were embarrassing comparisons. A huge illuminated Bible was opened to the family history page where births, deaths, and marriages had been duly recorded with a flourish. An heirloom silver chalice tipped against an Arthur Court bunny tray crossed with a Kirk's Rose baby spoon.

This bay window display was an eclectic mix of Then and Now. Unusual. Intriguing. Thought provoking. One could focus on any item and be lost for a pleasant time conjecturing beginnings, symbolism, usage, artistry, and value. While each item had its own intrinsic appeal, our window-shopping group easily shifted conversation from pleasant things to pleasant times. And there was a lesson in almost everything.

For example, a cage, however simple or elaborate, sparked the childhood memory of a baby bird falling from its nest. This tragedy required a valiant, whole-family effort to save the small bird's life through medicine-dropper feedings and a safe, makeshift nest of cotton batting. How precious are God's creatures!

The necklace called to mind the fascinating rise and fall of gem-quality beads bouncing on the ample bosom of someone's "ancient Aunt Lydia" as she labored up temple steps to pose for a family wedding picture.

The vintage Bible stirred up a vision of Grandfather reading out loud in a slow, sweet tone the Christmas story from his treasured tome. Everyone *lived* that silent, holy night.

The chalice was like the one searched for as a gift for the occasion of a twelve-year-old becoming a deacon and preparing to pass the sacrament of the Lord's Supper.

Pleasant times are . . . well . . . pleasant! Contemplating nature's creations, man's cleverness, and early memories is heart warming. However, a spectator's life is not satisfying, no matter how intriguing the "window" is. Many people hunger to *feel* something even more. They yearn for an *experience* with God. Spiritual experiences enrich life. A spiritual assurance of God's presence in our lives deepens with experience. Christ has said, "Be glad, for I am in your midst" (D&C 29:5).

Surely we understand that just because someone is apple-pie good, strictly obedient, and conscientiously toeing God's marked path every minute, there is no assurance that they will be spared trouble or that there won't be chances to be proven, to suffer, to grow and learn! By design man is faced with choices and adventures that point up the bitter and the sweet. Peter says: "Beloved [that means each of us too!], think it not strange concerning the fiery trial which is to try you, as though some strange thing happened unto you: but rejoice, inasmuch as ye are partakers of Christ's sufferings; that, when his glory shall be revealed [when Jesus shows his smiling face], ye may be glad also with exceeding joy" (1 Peter 4:12–13).

Any experience, from pleasant window-shopping to soul-wrenching repentance, that is God oriented, Christ focused, and perceived as eternal is not shallow. When we focus so, we will know joy and gladness and closeness to deity regardless of the "window dressing" of our lives or the descriptive details of our adventures in suffering, sinning, repenting, remembering, and receiving the Holy Ghost.

Elizabeth was divorced and the mother of three small children when she sinned (which translated means buckled, caved in, forgot Christ, forgot her covenants, and gave in to her frustrations of loneliness and rejection), succumbing to the lure of a rascal Church elder. She became pregnant and was shocked to discover that he had never had any intention of marrying her. He had merely used her for his personal gratification. He cared nothing about the child she was carrying and announced, in a cavalier way, "This is your problem." So her suffering was unilateral, eased only by placing the baby for adoption and by repentance. Regret was Elizabeth's from the first moment of her tragic mistake. The peace of a full repentance came only with her cultivation of a relationship with the Lord. Once she learned the saving power of God and the miracle of regaining the companionship of the Holy Ghost (which only can dwell in a clean soul), she became a woman of spirituality. Her other children were carefully taught, reared to righteousness with God in their midst. Each grew to serve a mission, to help others find the way to such full joy and gladness.

Leonard confessed, after his sinful action, that he fell because he was not prepared for the degree of temptation he suffered. He'd never felt anything like it before. Even though he had been a bishop and known the sweetness of guidance through the power of the Holy Ghost, he was overwhelmed by the cunning, "reasonable need" presented him by the devil. And as Leonard said, "I did eat!" (That's a moment to get all your antennae up!)

Even personal experience in dealing with people in trouble had not prepared Leonard sufficiently for the heartbreak that was his. The anguish he and all of his own family suffered was incredible and seemed interminable for a time. He said, "I had never really understood the depth and extent of suffering possible following excommunication until I experienced it. How my eyes were opened! How acute my compassion became—after the fact—for those troubled Saints I'd served as bishop! Nor had I valued the principles of the gospel and the path to peace and fulfillment as much as when I'd fallen out of sync. I wanted another chance. I wanted to turn my grief and sin into strength and effectiveness in helping others."

Leonard was a bright, charming, professional man with a large and lovely family. He didn't allow an encounter with the adversary to ruin his life and his family. For years he painfully, exactingly, diligently worked his way back into good standing among ward members, and he recaptured the circle of his family. He served in humble, exemplary ways. Some hid their tears when he passed the sacrament on Sunday with the deacons or collected fast offerings again, by choice as well as assignment.

Then the day came when indeed God was in our midst—when Jesus showed his smiling face. Leonard stood before his "support system" of ward members and in tears of happiness announced that his blessings had been restored and that he had gone back to the house of the Lord. With great emotion and a mood of incredible wonder he said, "What joy! What gladness fills my soul! How I love the Lord! Such love I have never felt from God nor has love like this flowed from me toward my fellowmen until I paid this high price and the Lord blessed me!"

Everyone was weeping through smiles as Leonard spoke, not only because of what he said but because we could see his radiance. We felt God in him. When his wife stood up next, tears flowed again. We witnessed the miracle of forgiveness. Many were strengthened by her joyous expressions of real love and gratitude for her husband and for proof of the Lord's gifts and goodness.

In our quest for perfection, often we gratefully just plod along the path of progress. We mean well. But as Leonard's story reminds us, good intentions aren't enough. "Yes. Yes!" "I'll give it my all, I will do my best" are worn phrases that need strengthening, it seems to me, by a spine and mind made sturdy through abiding closeness to the Lord. We will be helped if we allow him to be in our every waking thought, if we allow him to take lead of our thought and our behavior for the day, if we allow him to trigger our remembrance of precious, saving covenants. Our thoughts need to focus automatically, really, on the entreaties "What would Jesus have me do?" and "Who needs me now, Lord?" and "Bind my weaknesses in the whole armour of God against the tireless efforts of Satan" and "What must I do to have Jesus in the midst of my life, to have his smiling face always before me?"

Talk and think about pleasant times. What could be more pleasant than what these words bring to mind: "Lift up your hearts and be glad, for I am in your midst, and am your advocate with the Father; and it is his good will to give you the kingdom" (D&C 29:5). It is a superb ritual of gladness to deliberately set aside time to recall the pleasant times when Christ was in our midst.

Mother's Day has its special delights, but when the children do their sing thing, they outshine anything else. On a recent Mother's Day, the people who arrived early for sacrament meeting were a truly privileged part of the rehearsal proceedings. Fifty children—wiggling, jumping, poking, pushing, shoving, turning, talking, laughing, scratching, coughing, waving, changing the numbers on the song board, making rabbit ears on the innocent on the row ahead, and flipping the folding seats up and down, up and down—were far more interested in finding their parents in the congregation than in responding to the chorister. The rehearsal indicated a colossal flop. But when it was time for the opening prayer, these chosen children of the latter-days, this royal generation of well-taught, charming, destroying angels, were reverent! And then when it was their turn to sing, there wasn't a dry eye or casual spirit in the chapel. They were shining lights, touched by heaven, enhanced by the Spirit, and fully aware of their responsibility to make the day marvelous for Mother! Gladness filled our hearts that the Lord, indeed, is in the midst of little children on such an errand.

A Young Women class in Germany was an interesting mix of daughters of American military personnel and native girls. There were ten or twelve who were fourteen years old. In many ways this class was typical of classes of that age group meeting throughout the Church. The girls are at different levels of development physically and emotionally. Their social skills vary. Though Church members all with the same guiding goals for their Young Women programs, they are quick to form "safe" relationships through selective choice. Naturally some are left out and feel hurt. In this particular class there was an additional awkwardness among this age group because of their backgrounds and nationalities. The well-meaning teacher had visual aids and many papers before her that spoke of her conscientious preparation for the class, but she was having a very difficult time getting the girls' attention for her lesson. In fact, I have rarely been part of such an experience where the girls were so outspoken in their rudeness to each other. The American girls were not welcome, it was clear. It was also evident that the German girls, on the other hand, did not measure up to the American girls' standards of teenage chic!

The teacher tried several times to bring a unity of focus but without success. She folded her hands on the scriptures in her lap and offered a silent prayer for heavenly support, even intervention. A few moments later she felt inspired to call one of the ringleaders forward. Together they stood before the disgruntled group, the sweet teacher's arm lightly around her young friend. At first the other girls paid little attention, but then they realized that the young woman was being paid a tribute by her teacher. When the teacher finished, the girl was smiling broadly. Then the teacher issued classroom instructions: they would start at each end of the class circle and alternately work their way forward as each in turn said something nice about the girl across the circle. Now a wonderful thing happened. The girls busied themselves trying to think of something nice to say about a girl who was *not* sitting beside them. This demand for positive input worked. The hearts of the girls proved kind. They were thoughtful and generous rather than immature and thoughtless. In moments the whole spirit of the meeting changed. It was a miracle to witness such an immediate answer to prayer, for the Spirit descended upon that class, Christ was in their midst, and everyone was glad! It was a most amazing exchange of love and awakening of friendship and understanding. One American girl hugged the teacher after class and tearfully told her that she had vowed this would be her last time to make the effort to be part of this group. She had hated it before. She had only come that day because of a "deal" she'd made with her parents to try again. Now there was a holy spirit of healing in the room and of identity for every unique girl. They had a door opened for knowing and appreciating each other.

For a fiftieth wedding anniversary celebration one family planned activities that retraced their family's history. Included was a time in the temple with every one of the children and their spouses present. The oldest daughter, who was single, had readied herself to join the family for this special time. You see, she had been pursuing her career in various parts of the country, and in the tradition of the day, she had been encouraged to wait until she was to be married before getting her own endowment. The advice begged the question, "Why should endowments be postponed until marriage?" However, she kept up her hope and Church activity. But the years passed and she didn't get married. As a result, she missed the temple weddings of her siblings and cousins, as well as the sealings of adopted children to some of her family members. Finally, for this wedding anniversary celebration, she made the decision to go to the temple and be part of it. Oh, the joy of that family day! Not a chair was empty—underscoring the promise of a complete heavenly reunion. The understanding came into each *imperfect, striving* soul that Christ was in their midst. He was pleased with that family circle individually and collectively. This gave direction and impetus to the days ahead. Life wasn't over; it was just beginning in its fullest sense.

It was a privilege to be part of a gathering of women, hosted and arranged by lovely Sally Grant in the stunning setting of Chase and Grethe Peterson's mountain home. Many were women whose lives had brought them to that valley for a fresh start. Past painful problems and heartbreak were figuratively buried in the pure white of high ski slopes and in valleys blanketed in wildflowers. Benevolence enhanced these women with upturned faces catching spring sun. Incredible compassion and practical helpfulness was evident among them, because each had been through the proverbial Life War. Varied in the details of age, advantages, financial situation, and marital bliss (or not), trouble was their common denominator. Yet, rare in gatherings of women, there was *no* judging, gossiping, guessing, or embellishing. Nor was cruel coolness evident. Christ was in our midst. We were glad for this and for each other.

It was a prominent viewing before the funeral of a prominent citizen. Everybody was there, so to speak. It was, in fact, a most familiar Mormon-culture scene—people loving people. Then a wonderful exchange occurred, which was noted by some with wonderful amazement. A woman waiting in line was approached by a woman just leaving. There, before many who knew of their severe situation of estrangement, a miracle happened as a gospel principle was played out. There was a formal greeting, then the one who had been cruelly offended looked into the eyes of the woman still in line, who was her offender. Suddenly she wrapped her arms close about her thoughtless "friend," and they shared the healing mix of repentance and forgiveness. The offender was so overcome she cried out (loud enough that others could hear), "Oh, thank you, thank you! I have needed this moment."

Sometimes we can't control what happens to us. Our goal should be to control the way we respond to hurt, mistakes, ill health, or stress, for instance. In a special setting at Brigham Young University, President Rex Lee said, "I have concluded that I can set goals till the cows come home, but there are things that come into my life that are totally unanticipated." The discussion that followed centered on the critical need for the Lord to be in our midst to help us through challenges of health and happiness.

We all have been blessed in so many needful, small ways that we know Christ is in our midst. Look for the small miracles, the surprising answers to prayers. We don't always know God's purposes in delaying or denying us the big miracles, but when we recognize the small, wonderful proof of his love, we almost question why he bothers with small concerns. But he does bother! We are suddenly flooded with awareness that he lives, loves us, knows our anguish, and helps us get through the trouble that we must go through for whatever reason. Oh, how we need to have God in our midst—in our head, in our heart, in our vision of the world, in our love for each other, in our daily labor to sustain our families and improve society!

The Lord keeps his promises and he waits to be gracious. The awesome bonus for us in this remarkable link to heaven comes through the Lord as he says: "Lift up your hearts and be glad, for I am in your midst, and am your advocate with the Father; and it is his good will to give you the kingdom" (D&C 29:5). And there is more! The Lord then goes on to say that anything we ask for in faith, being united in prayer according to his command, we shall receive! (See verse 6.) This is possible because of his goodness, his power, his urgent desire that we be gathered together in the presence of our Heavenly Father. What remains, then, is for us to live so that the Lord will always be in our midst, so that we can sing our song, emphasizing that when Jesus shows his smiling face there is sunshine in the soul.

11

Jesus Listening Can Hear

This book takes its title from one of the great older hymns. It has the tempo instruction *joyfully*. This hymn is not a lament, nor is it about trying to send prayers past the ceiling. It is not a dirge of doubt about whether anybody Up There is paying any attention at all. This is a sunshine song of gladness springing from a heart full of faith that "Jesus listening can hear." He not only hears and listens, but he is aware of the "song [you] cannot sing." That is a comforting idea to review before a prayer is ever initiated. Yes, he lives, he listens to prayers "uttered or unexpressed," he cares, *and* with him nothing is impossible.

I believe this with all my heart. That's why there is sunshine in my soul.

We are glad when our prayers are answered according to our pleas. Even when the Lord's will and not ours is done, there can be a sweet gladness that fills the soul because we know that God is good, wise, and wants the best for us. Ultimately we see that trusting God is truly better than getting our own way. After all, his wisdom is grander and promises greater gladness than our own. There are many, many times, of course, when we are overwhelmed that our prayers are not only answered according to the desires of our hearts but that God has anticipated our needs and planned wonderful surprises!

President Ezra Taft Benson, who at one time was the United States Secretary of Agriculture, has been given credit for the statement about wise farmers: "The value of a man is evidenced by the dust on his knees." Good people of whatever formal religious affiliation have always sought a higher power in submissive, contemplative meditation.

Some years ago during the study of the Old Testament in our Gospel Doctrine class, I did some private reading of the text. Class discussions are interesting, but when looking for personal answers to current needs and for a strengthening feeling of trust in the flow of life, I have found that it pays off to dig out the truth from the word itself. For example, the Old Testament treatment of prayer was a subject with which I was least familiar. So I crammed the prayer theme: Adam and Eve calling "upon the name of the Lord" after being cast out of the garden; father Abraham crying out to the Lord when Isaac lay bound on an improvised altar; Moses on the mount learning about holiness to the Lord and the laws governing man's relationships with God and all people; David's explanation to Saul that the Lord who delivered him (David) out of the lion's paw would also deliver him out of the hand of Goliath the Philistine. The thing about studying the Old Testament is that one gets the feeling that God was *real* to the people. And approachable. God's children *conversed* with him. They expected God to listen. They did not doubt but what he'd be with them when he was needed.

At the time of this deep study I was carrying the heavy burden of a strange illness that baffled doctors. Diagnosis was elusive. My research was to find how to get answers to prayers for guidance and help. So thorough had been my preparations to go before Heavenly Father, that the prayer themes in the New Testament, Book of Mormon, Doctrine and Covenants, and the Pearl of Great Price seemed as familiar to me as my recipe for brownies—and I could make brownies blindfolded.

With the subject of prayer, I needed a fresh viewpoint, a reinforcement of what I already had been taught or had experienced. I needed a review, at least, of what God has said through his prophets on the subject of prayer. I searched for examples, prototypes, paradigms. I found such perspective in Hezekiah.

When Hezekiah was sick unto death, the prophet Isaiah came to him and said, "Thus saith the Lord, Set thine house in order; for thou shalt die, and not live."

This isn't exactly what Hezekiah had in mind. "Set your house in order!" It sounded familiar to me! When one of the Lord's anointed speaks to a family in crisis his words are taken seriously. Hezekiah was heartbroken at Isaiah's words. I was fascinated now and anxious to find out what happened next.

What did he do about this? In his sick bed Hezekiah found privacy for secret prayer by turning his face to the wall and beseeching the Lord. The account continues: "O Lord, remember now how I have walked before thee in truth and with a perfect heart, and have done that which is good in thy sight. And Hezekiah wept sore."

Before Isaiah had left the premises, he was prompted by the Lord to return to the room of Hezekiah and tell him that the God of David had heard his prayer—that God had said, "I have seen thy tears: behold, I will heal thee: on the third day thou shalt go up unto the house of the Lord."

Later, Hezekiah said to Isaiah, "Good is the word of the Lord which thou hast spoken. . . . Is it not good, if peace and truth be in my days?" Hezekiah was humbled and then motivated! (2 Kings 20:1–5, 19.)

Just for the record, Hezekiah did much good in his remaining days. He was a religious and political reformer. He is famous for building a conduit tunnel which brought water within the walls of Jerusalem about 701 B.C. It is a remarkable engineering feat that is still in use today. Note: if ever you get to Istanbul you can see the original inscription carved in stone at the time of the completion of this tunnel that was dug in a zig-zag course from each end until the workmen met. (See LDS Bible Dictionary, p. 702.)

It is a rare person who hasn't pursued prayer. However secret or public the prayer, people need and want help from a higher power. I believe that when help is sought

God helps people on whatever spiritual level they have reached—blessings and answers are commensurate with effort, agency, agenda, and God's will. However, it seems to me that effective praying—that is, actually reaching God through a one-on-one communication and experiencing a feeling of an exchange of love with him—happens according to law, formula, recipe, pattern, principles.

It is the law of the harvest. The farmer who plants corn doesn't expect to harvest peas or peaches. The person who cries out frantically for handouts from heaven but has not personally prepared may indeed be disappointed.

There is an additional mature perspective that has to do with attitude: Like the words in Miss Marple's English flower garden, "Cheer up or get dug up!"

If my college English courses serve me correctly, it was the venerable Chaucer who wrote:

> Whoever prays must fast, he must keep clean,
> Fatten his soul and make his body lean.
> (*The Canterbury Tales* [New York: Penguin
> Books, 1988], p. 327.)

In the process of "fattening" the soul, the following simple but serious exercise can help.

Ask yourself:

How do I feel about God?

What do I know of his goodness?

Do I believe that he can help me as well as the prophet? Does he know something I don't know that impacts the outcome of cries for help?

Then isn't his will better than mine?

Though you find your own strength from the prophet and from scriptural passages that speak God's truth in terms you understand, I have chosen to include excerpts from a magnificent Psalm: "Have mercy upon me, O God, according to thy lovingkindness: according unto the multitude of thy tender mercies blot out my transgressions. Wash me thoroughly from mine iniquity, and cleanse me from my sin. For I acknowledge my transgressions. . . . Make me to hear joy and gladness. . . . Create in me a clean heart, O God; and renew a right spirit within me." (Psalm 51:1–3, 8–10.)

As you exercise faith in Christ through your need, self-discipline, and righteousness, you not only will become an even better person but your faith will increase. The following is a true account of an incident which I witnessed, and I have written it as accurately as I could, to catch the fact and spirit of what happened. There are many fine lessons to consider in this story.

She stood in fast and testimony meeting one fall day, a neighbor we'd known long and admired. Her hands, curled over the pew against which she leaned, showed the comfortable evidence of hard work in life. Her hair now was nearly all white, only peppered with dark on the springy, wiry strands casually knotted on the crown of her head. She spoke in a gentle, well-modulated voice, and her bright eyes reflected her intelligent interest in things. Anna spoke matter-of-factly when she said, "I would like the children of this ward to hear the story of the miracle of the pear tree. It is a true story that happened to me this year. It was my pear tree.

"Most of you know where I live. It has been our family home for forty years. There we struggled with our trials and welcomed our joys. And the pear tree was one of my joys. When the children were young we were having our trials. It was hard getting enough food for growing young bodies. We had planted a Bartlett pear tree. Our front yard had the best sun exposure, and so that tree grew right from the grassy stretch of parking between the street and sidewalk. We watched it flourish and produce more pears each year. It gave us hope and gladness all those years. It also gave us pears.

"But for a long time that pear tree has been nothing more than a nuisance. Those of you who walk by our house might have wondered why I didn't cut it down. The budding fruit, hard like little rocks, would drop all over the ground and sidewalk. People would trip over them or turn an ankle. The fallen pears would clutter the gutter, creating a backlog of debris that caused floods in rainstorms.

"One day this past spring my spirits were so low that I got myself out of the house. I walked toward the pear tree and wept a bit as I recalled the fruitful years when bottled pears had pleasured our lives and given us sustenance. Suddenly, my need for sustenance right then was so great that I bowed my head and prayed. Then I looked up into heaven and quietly sang out, 'O God, bless the pear tree! Bless the pear tree that it may yield good fruit.' And now I have forty quarts of bottled pears on the shelves in my basement. And I wanted the children of this ward to hear about the miracle of the pear tree so that they would know that God lives and answers prayers."

That same evening we were invited to a social gathering with people who had been in the congregation at fast and testimony meeting. Someone raised a question about the "miracle of the pear tree." The discussion was lively and the mood was decidedly skeptical. "She probably pruned and watered the old pear tree, gave it a shot or two of fertilizer," observed a well-known attorney. Similar comments from other distinguished citizens were tossed on the Discredit Heap.

I was annoyed at what was going on. Hadn't any of these people ever been close enough to the Spirit to recognize the faith of this woman? I took courage and spoke up. "All right. Show of hands—how many of us pruned and watered and fertilized our pear trees this year?" Several hands were raised. "And how many of you were blessed with a bumper crop of pears—worth forty quarts?"

All hands dropped to laps as people looked about at each other in astonishment. Nobody in that neighborhood had any pears. Though we had pruned and watered, there was no miracle in our own orchards because a killer frost had nipped our fruit trees in the bud last spring.

When true faith is present, God blesses with miracles, with ministering angels, with spiritual gifts, with every conceivable good thing. Our prayers are heard and noted, and signs follow the believers!

A beautiful young woman from South America was thinking about serious matters when she was supposed to be shopping. She had a life-changing decision to make and her mind was spinning. She stood before a sweeping array of vegetables in the produce section of the amazing supermarket. She stroked the ruddy carrots. She let her finger slide down the shiny, slick green of a cucumber. She cupped the fat mushrooms in her hand then lightly rippled her palm over the fluffy salad greens. Approvingly, and with a kind of wonder as well, Magali scanned the wide range of vegetables from snap beans to artichokes, red radish balls to warty squash. And cabbage—what a remarkable invention the cabbage was, round after round of leaves pressed tightly against themselves into a large crisp ball!

Suddenly Magali marveled at God's creativity. There was nourishment for the body and beauty for the soul right here in the produce section, and she hadn't even considered the fruits yet!

If God could make all this, Magali reasoned, as well as creatures of the sea, the sky, the deep earth and leave nothing unattended or wanting, he could come up with a plan for man that would offer the abundant life and the road back to heaven. After all, man was his most marvelous creation.

Magali looked at her own hand holding a vegetable. That hand could do a multitude of things and was a miracle itself! Surely the Creator himself could prepare a perfect plan for mankind to follow. The missionaries had explained to Magali that the Church claimed God had done just that and that this plan came complete with principles and protective commandments to help people.

Magali was still thoughtful as she looked at the cobs of corn wrapped tightly in their own protective husks. Even husks had multiple uses! A miracle, really. God's doing. She closed her eyes in secret prayer, clutching the cobs of corn, "O God, I thank you for the corn . . . husks and all!"

Suddenly, Magali turned from the produce display without making a selection. She pushed the shopping cart to the door, parked it, and resolutely walked outside to the pay phone. She dropped her coin in the slot and dialed the number of the stake missionary couple who had been teaching her the gospel. She knew her prayers had been answered and she wanted to tell them about it. With pounding heart and tear-filled eyes she waited. When they answered, Magali almost blurted the words, "This is Magali. I do believe! When can I be baptized?"

Everyone was glad about that.

Stacey's answer to prayer has brought her joy to this day. It all began when she was twelve, and today she is a mother of two very beautiful answers to prayer. Stacey's family had become inactive in the Church and had moved a great deal. Her life at twelve was an emotional swing. She'd make friends and lose them. She would attend a Church meeting with one and learn something that struck her as truth, and then she would be snatched out of that environment. There was little support at home and no answers for the longings of her heart. Explanations about the gospel were dissatisfying and reluctantly given.

The family was moving again when Stacey's prayers to Heavenly Father changed. They were no longer recited pieces of thought carried over from her early childhood. The family did not say prayers of any kind in the home now, but Stacey wanted more out of life. She wanted to be happy again and actively growing in the gospel. And she wanted it so much that her prayers changed. She didn't define it this way at the time, but she recognizes the change now—she went before Heavenly Father with a broken heart and a humble and contrite spirit. Her nightly prayer for a time was a passionate plea which included three elements: she wanted to be a good girl so that she would be worthy to associate with people active in the Church; she needed help because she didn't know how to go about getting what she wanted; and she wanted to know that God loved her.

Almost before the week was over, and after the family was in their new home, a Young Women leader called at their home and Stacey's life was joyful! Stacey was glad again. Stacey was caught up in happy pursuits of personal progress. She even participated in the Churchwide banner-making project and marched in the Days of '47 Parade with fifteen hundred other young women dressed in white displaying their homemade banners on tall poles. I saw Stacey at the beginning of the preparations for the event, and she was one miserable girl. But there were people standing by to help her. She herself felt hope and God's love, and she poured out her heart during the speech contest. She was selected—partly in response to a prompting we felt from the Spirit! There were so many to choose from, but Stacey's name wouldn't leave my heart. By the time she delivered her speech in the public event, she was a different girl.

Stacey to this day speaks of her gratitude for secret prayer and for leaders who believe in promptings of the Spirit. Prayers are answered. Stacey married very young in the temple to a returned missionary, and their life conforms to the joy-bringing life God promises to the obedient.

One important part of the Latter-day Saint way is to back up ideas with scripture. If a thought can be substantiated by a scripture, then it can be taken seriously. We learn in the Book of Mormon that people can pray to God wherever they might be. Secret prayer can happen on one's knees, in the produce department, or while standing beneath a pear tree, for instance. Zenos, an ancient prophet quoted by Alma, said: "Thou art merciful, O God, for thou hast heard my prayer, even when I was in the wilderness; yea, thou wast merciful when I prayed concerning those who were mine enemies. . . . Thou wast merciful unto me when I did cry unto thee in my field. . . . When I did turn to my house thou didst hear me in my prayer. . . . Thou hast . . . heard my cries in the midst of thy congregations. . . . And thou hast also heard me when I have been cast out and have been despised. . . ; yea, thou didst hear my cries. . . . And thou didst hear me because of mine afflictions and my sincerity." (Alma 33:4, 5, 6, 9, 10, 11.)

Pray in your secret places! Pray in sincerity, for a prayer admits gratitude for the joy and gladness in life, for the wonders of creation, for the amazing goodness and beauty of God's children, for comfort and strength, and for supportive "other" blessings that come even when prayers are answered in a way different from what we had in mind.

A season ago, our lovely daughter was fighting for her life. Her disease was one of the strange new ones that would not be diagnosed until the autopsy was performed. She did not want to die. She had a young family. She had a satisfying and important Church calling and a beautiful new home. She had faith and she engaged in a great deal of secret prayer. She sought anointing and administration from the priesthood.

During an illness it often helps to be engaged in a project to keep the mind occupied and the hours in bed profitable, and this young mother used her enviable creative skills to work her belief into a pillow. "Do Not Doubt!" she boldly worked in beautiful needlepoint letters across the canvas. In her hospital room, that pillow had a place of honor for all to see—beloved nurses, honored doctors, technicians, visitors, and her family. She'd tried to get her life in order to be worthy of the miracle. And she did not doubt. She was claiming her blessings—as she wanted them. Now she thought that all she had to do was be patient until the miracle happened.

As she steadily worsened, I became very concerned. I wondered if she would die being angry at God, and I couldn't stand that. My own prayers changed then. I prayed for God's will in the matter of her sickness and her lifespan agenda, of course. But now I also prayed fervently for a light to fill her, that whatever the outcome, it would be recognized as a blessing and the will of God. *That* prayer of mine was answered. In a very sacred moment our daughter was caught up in the Spirit and allowed to discuss the timing of her death and its purpose. I was with her and saw her transfigured, if you will. She was filled with light, and never in her life was she more lovely and radiant. She lived three or four more months in peaceful acceptance and in an attitude of preparation for leaving her family and moving on.

There is a definition of prayer in the LDS Bible Dictionary that is important to note as we try to understand the avenue to God that is ours: "Prayer is the act by which the will of the Father and the will of the child are brought into correspondence with each other. The object of prayer is not to change the will of God, but to secure for ourselves and for others blessings that God is already willing to grant, but that are made conditional on our asking for them. Blessings require some work or effort on our part before we can obtain them. Prayer is a form of work, and is an appointed means for obtaining the highest of all blessings." (Pp. 752–53.)

We know God lives and hears our prayers. Perhaps we don't always realize this wonder in our lives, because often we are looking for some other blessing than that which we have at hand. The privilege of sacred prayer is to draw close to God. He already knows the desires of our hearts, but a change must occur within us; having been passive we become active through prayer. Prayer is, indeed, a boon for us. For a choice lift, sing again the old-fashioned, heart-warming lines:

> There is an hour of peace and rest,
> Unmarred by earthly care;
> 'Tis when before the Lord I go,
> And kneel in secret prayer.
>
> May my heart be turned to pray,
> Pray in secret day by day,
> That this boon to mortals giv'n
> May unite my soul with heav'n.
>
> (Hans Henry Petersen, "Secret Prayer,"
> *Hymns,* no. 144.)

Being united with heaven is what gladness is really all about. When this condition exists, regardless of the terrifying or stressful details of life, everything will ultimately be happy and fine. We go before the Lord faithfully and cheerfully, and Jesus listening can hear!

12

Happy Endings

Is it all right to figuratively wave good-bye to you, the reader? You see, to me there is something exceedingly tender about an ending, a closing, a good-bye before separation after a relationship, an occasion, or a shared experience. That includes the ending of a book shared between an author and the reader to whom she reveals her soul.

A proper happy ending—a wave or kiss good-bye, a few stems of flowers in farewell—has ever been so among many I've met over the years. When we were being driven away from the mission home in Helsinki, Finland, Sister Beverly Benson Parker, an instinctively hospitable hostess, stood on the broad porch steps and waved to us. In delight I waved back, of course. Here was another "waver," and I loved it! I kept watching and waving, as did she. She even moved from the steps to the curb, to keep us in sight longer. It was a memorable and happy ending to our assignment in Helsinki.

Jane Howard said that her mother always waved to their tenants upstairs as they drove off to work. If the tenant neglected to wave back she took it personally. Jane commented, "Not everybody, it was clear, came from such a long line of wavers as we did. 'Wave to the pine trees,' our Aunt Frances would instruct us. 'They always wave back.'"

What was it like when we left heaven? How will it be when we leave earth? Some gifted people have such a charming way to say farewell-until-later. For example, Lowell M. Durham Jr. waxed eloquent and tender for his father, a professor and news media music critic of some acclaim. During Dr. Durham's mission days in Britain he became director of the Millennial Chorus, and this group entertained us in our community for several decades. We came to love Lowell! And his son, as well, who authored these farewell lines when his father died:

> When I was young,
> I thought the music came through
> Those elegant hands, first left,
> Then right, up the keys
> Playing "Danny Boy,"
> Till I was filled with tears and calm
> As he brought life to the music room.
>
> At choir, left hand poised in air,
> Head down, he conjured from
> East Millcreek voices
> Milton's "far blazing beam of majesty,"
> Using spells flung from his fingers
> Like explosions from Merlin's wand.
>
> Now, with him gone,
> There is a dusky silence of a kind
> I'll use for remembering.
> Yet I'll still have my father's blessing,
> Surely not his explosions of light and sound,
> But just some slight, tingling magic,
> In my fingertips.

When the choral group sang "Let Nothing Ever Grieve Thee," conducted by another son, Tom Durham, it seemed possible to have happiness even in the wrenching separation of death, even with all of its promise of reunion.

The Prophet Joseph Smith functioned in an aura of incredible inspiration from God. While this may not have been a constant condition, evidence in Joseph's teachings and our long perspective prove this point for us. So many great truths have been poured upon the generations since his mission of the restoration of the gospel! One of the most important for us to consider as we close this book is that Joseph really had a handle on happy endings for the daily dozen of problems and choices as well as for the final outcome of life. He said, "Happiness is the object and design of our existence; and will be the end thereof, if we pursue the path that leads to it; and this path is virtue, uprightness, faithfulness, holiness, and keeping all the commandments of God" (*Teachings of the Prophet Joseph Smith,* sel. Joseph Fielding Smith [Salt Lake City: Deseret Book Co., 1938], pp. 255–56).

Those are words you might expect and even be familiar with, but now consider this practical and motivating perspective: "As God has designed our happiness . . . He never will institute an ordinance or give a commandment to His people that is not calculated in its nature to promote that happiness which He has designed, and which will not end in the greatest amount of good and glory to those who become the recipients of His law and ordinances" (*Teachings of the Prophet Joseph Smith,* pp. 256–57).

There, we can have the brightest sunshine in our souls because of our faith. It is part of the plan, and our holy right, to choose happy endings to our solutions to problems, to the days of our time, and indeed, to life itself. Viktor E. Frankl, describing his grinding years in a concentration camp, said: "I told my comrades (who lay motionless, although occasionally a sigh could be heard) that human life, under any circumstances, never ceases to have a meaning, and that this infinite meaning of life includes suffering and dying, privation and death. . . . I said that someone looks down on each of us in difficult hours—a friend, a wife, somebody alive or dead, or a God—and he would not expect us to disappoint him." Dr. Frankl sums up his philosophy in these words: "Everything can be taken from a man but one thing: the last of the human freedoms—to choose one's attitude in any given set of circumstances." (*Man's Search for Meaning* [New York: Pocket Books, 1984], pp. 104, 86.)

It is my understanding of a story surrounding four lines by radiantly melancholy Emily Dickinson that the verse grew from a question put to her about how happiness is at last attained:

> I gained it so,
> By climbing slow,
> By catching at the twigs that grow
> Between the bliss and me.

Mark and Caroline caught their bliss by catching and reconciling every distinction in their lives. Mature singles, they were lined up by a loving, wise older woman who knew them both. Caroline was the mother of five children all in a row. The youngest was still in grade school when the children's father announced his intention of not being part of the family anymore. It seems there was another woman. There was a divorce, and vast adjustment was required of this family betrayed by its patriarch and priesthood leader. And Caroline was now available for help in getting a new life established.

Mark's story was different. Like Caroline he was a significant, attractive, mature person with a life that hadn't turned out the way he had planned. He had waited long years for the satisfying relationship that had eluded him thus far. And he was childless. Mark and Caroline dated, they listened, they comforted, they struggled. They were absolutely attracted to each other, but with five children and complicated financial matters at stake, establishing an ideal LDS family seemed almost out of the question. During every step of the important path they were walking, each fasted, prayed, and went to the temple regarding personal needs and the grander outcome of a reconstituted family. As they worked through each separate concern, we watched their love grow and their personal lives change. Each was enhanced by an increased spiritual quality. Each made adjustments to accommodate the other's needs and obligations. Then finally, the temple wedding took place. At the altar knelt two people marvelously in love—fresh spirited and ready for each other in a union that promised near-perfection—not in spite of the five children but partly because of them. Weddings and missions and incredible joy marked the following years. "Our story has a happy ending," explained Mark, "even if these few sunshine years were the total consideration."

Then they invited Caroline's former mother-in-law to a missionary open house at their home for one of the children. Caroline explained to Mark that every time her ex-mother-in-law had talked to her since the divorce, the woman had sobbed over the turn of events. (Caroline wondered if she cried before her own offending son as well!) But, Caroline noted, the woman had been too stunned to cry as she checked out Mark and Caroline's beautiful home and family life.

Mark reported to Caroline a conversation he had with the former mother-in-law:

The woman said, "Ah . . . I've been watching you, sir, and watching the two of you together. You seem to be very much in love with each other."

"Yes, we are," Mark agreed politely.

"Are you happy?"

"Yes."

"Is Caroline happy?"

"Yes, my dear," Mark replied sensitively. "We are both very, very happy. It is right for us." And *then* once more the former mother-in-law cried.

Recently a handsome young doctor stood to share his feelings during fast and testimony meeting. He spoke of the happy ending to his wife's difficult pregnancy and his gratitude for her life and the joy they felt in their new baby girl. In the naming and blessing of the baby this young man had explained that her name would be Amilia Moira. She would be called Milly, but she was to remember that she had been named for two honored ancestors—strong branches of a family tree that made it possible for this baby to be born in a land of freedom and affluence under covenant and shelter of gospel truth.

On the other hand, Rod Johnson reported on the eye opening experience that made him question his own road to happiness in this land of affluence. He visited an island in

Tonga, where everybody was as happy as the people described in 4 Nephi. There was no crime, because there was nothing to steal. Nobody was sick or overweight, because their balanced diet came from the land itself and the fruit-bearing palm trees. Everybody was happy, and there was laughter in the very air. No wonder! They had nothing to break down, gas-up, overhaul, vacuum, or show off to the neighbors (who also had nothing of troublesome earthly goods). Brother Johnson said that since his return to the United States he had spent a lot of time wondering about the mixed blessings of affluence and envying those island people their simple, good, and happy life.

T. H. White, author of *The Once and Future King,* included these significant lines about what really brings a happy ending in all of life's situations: "'The best thing for being sad', replied Merlyn, beginning to puff and blow, 'is to learn something. That is the only thing that never fails. You may grow old and trembling in your anatomies, you may lie awake at night listening to the disorder of your veins, you may miss your only love, you may see the world about you devastated by evil lunatics, or know your honour trampled in the sewers of baser minds. There is only one thing for it then—to learn. Learn why the world wags and what wags it.'" (*The Once and Future King* [New York: Berkley Books, 1966], p. 183.) There will be few happy endings otherwise, and finding happiness is, after all, the silent goal of our lives.

Henry Ward Beecher wrote, "You recollect the story of the woman who, when her only child died, in rapture looking up, as with the face of an angel, said, 'I give you joy, my darling.'" That single sentence has gone with me years and years down through my life, quickening and comforting me. Even in death there can be a kind of happy ending because of the quality of faith and depth of understanding we are blessed with in the Church.

President Howard W. Hunter told a story in general conference, April 1992, which forever changed the perspective of hundreds of listeners. It seemed to be an ideal example of applying gospel principles to a difficult situation to bring forth a happy ending. He said: "After his father became ill, Vern

Crowley took responsibility for running the family wrecking yard although he was only fifteen years of age. Some customers occasionally took unfair advantage of the young man, and parts were disappearing from the lot overnight. Vern was angry and vowed to catch someone and make an example of him. Vengeance would be his.

"Just after his father had started to recover from his illness, Vern was making his rounds of the yard one night at closing time. It was nearly dark. In a distant corner of the property, he caught sight of someone carrying a large piece of machinery toward the back fence. He ran like a champion athlete and caught the young thief. His first thought was to take out his frustrations with his fists and then drag the boy to the front office and call the police. His heart was full of anger and vengeance. He had caught his thief, and he intended to get his just dues.

"Out of nowhere, Vern's father came along, put his weak and infirm hand on his son's shoulder, and said, 'I see you're a bit upset, Vern. Can I handle this?' He then walked over to the young would-be thief and put his arm around his shoulder, looked him in the eye for a moment, and said, 'Son, tell me, why are you doing this? Why were you trying to steal that transmission?' Then Mr. Crowley started walking toward the office with his arm around the boy, asking questions about the young man's car problems as they walked. By the time they had arrived at the office, the father said, 'Well, I think your clutch is gone and that's causing your problem.'

"In the meantime, Vern was fuming. 'Who cares about his clutch?' he thought. 'Let's call the police and get this over with.' But his father just kept talking. 'Vern, get him a clutch. Get him a throwout bearing, too. And get him a pressure plate. That should take care of it.' The father handed all of the parts to the young man who had attempted robbery and said, 'Take these. And here's the transmission, too. You don't have to steal, young man. Just ask for it. There's a way out of every problem. People are willing to help.'

"Brother Vern Crowley said he learned an everlasting lesson in love that day. The young man came back to the lot often. Voluntarily, month by month, he paid for all of the parts

Vic Crowley had given him, including the transmission. During those visits, he asked Vern why his dad was the way he was and why he did what he did. Vern told him something of their Latter-day Saint beliefs and how much his father loved the Lord and loved people. Eventually the would-be thief was baptized."

Now, that is a happy ending! President Hunter went on to point out that the whole world could benefit from such an example. He then quoted this passage of scripture: "Wherefore, whoso believeth in God might with surety hope for a better world. . . . In the gift of his Son hath God prepared a more excellent way." (Ether 12:4, 11.) ("A More Excellent Way," *Ensign,* May 1992, p. 62.)

Happy endings to very difficult situations draw forth a gratitude to God like almost nothing else. Along with gratitude there will be a flood of well-being, benevolence, and gladness. LaRue Longden told me that when her mother was dying her last instruction to her personable, delightful, beloved LaRue (who knew the value of spreading sunshine among her fellowmen) was to "lock one of your inimitable glad giggles inside my coffin!"

Ralph Hill was a great leader and team member. We cochaired the Church's observance for the nation's bicentennial celebration, and it was soon apparent to me that if *we* didn't have fun planning it there was little chance of anyone else's enjoying what we planned. Ralph insisted that there was to be gladness and an exchange of appreciation for each other among the standing committees. The happy ending of those labors was a tremendously successful event—so successful that the managers of the Salt Palace requested that our exhibits and our Heritage City (early Salt Lake revisited) be held over through the tourist season.

At Ralph's funeral, a great secret to his success was revealed: "Ralph focused on the process not the problem, right to the end. His philosophy was to do all you can and then stand still and wait with utmost assurance for the salvation of God." He believed that happy endings, relief, restitution, triumph came through this attitude of "utmost assurance," and he often referred to D&C 121:8–9: "And then, if thou endure it well, God shall exalt thee on high. . . . Thy friends do stand by thee, and they shall hail thee again with warm hearts and friendly hands." Yes! Yes!

Sometimes bringing a happy ending to a tough situation requires more than endurance and faith in God. Taking hold of one's life and seasoning it with a positive attitude can change dark into sunshine, sadness into happy moments. During one waiting period at the Salt Lake International Airport I was reminded of this again. I sat next to a Korean girl who had married a Caucasian pilot she met in Japan. They had converted to the Church and then finally moved back to Utah. Now they were waiting for her parents to arrive for a visit. The parents spoke no English, and the girl confidentially revealed to me that she was seriously considering taking her babies and going back to Korea with her parents. You see—even in this day and age—her husband's family had never accepted her. Though she had learned English well, they assumed that she not only didn't have a grasp of the language but that she was deaf and dumb as well. Plus, she was so different that they had nothing in common, not even the gospel of Jesus Christ, which they espoused and to which she had converted. She was snubbed by the ward members in the humble community in which she lived—a community where the people had found their own way of showing discrimination by shunning this well-educated, classy, beautiful Asian girl. It seemed there was no way for a happy ending for that little family.

We talked long because the incoming plane was late. We focused on the idea that some people serve mankind and the Lord by hanging in there as examples, forerunners, pacesetters, hanging in there to break prejudice and tradition. Thus they can make happy endings possible for others who will follow. By the time the girl's mother and father arrived, my family and I were Latter-day Saint, English-speaking friends of their daughter, and we helped to welcome them to our world. Soon there was laughter over sign language, a smile on the young wife's face, and joy in the meeting of grandparents and grandchildren who had never seen each other before. By that time the young husband had decided to show up. Now everything was going to be all right.

117

My daughters Susan and Carla teamed together to prepare for me an organized "happy days calendar." It wasn't like the time-planning organizer I used to find valuable in a previous stage of life. This calendar was structured so that each week I could record glad happenings. In this handsome three-ring binder that Susan had covered in gorgeous paisley fabric there was also room behind each week's entry to add proof of happy happenings—greeting cards, birth announcements, graduation invitations, gift enclosures, wedding photographs, class reunion mementos. Now when the dawn brings dark days or the night-lights burn with care-giving, I can turn to a happy day and remember the goodness of God and people helping people.

John Culhane has made it a practice to record on his happiness calendar any exhilarating sights of nature, such as the spouting gray whales he saw off the coast of California in a scene so beautiful it made his heart leap. And it leaps again when he looks back and rereads such an entry. He makes it a practice to jot down enough facts to secure the memory of special-occasion days too, or lessons he's learned from the great or the simple people he's written news stories about.

An absolutely fantastic ending for the career of Dan Jansen, American Olympic speed skater, came when he competed for the gold medal in the 1994 Winter Games. According to media reports, all of America and beyond watched when, after years of heartbreak and struggle, endless worries and injuries and failures, Dan won his gold medal and set a world record. With his eyes shining with joy and his little daughter, eight-month-old Jane, bundled in his arms, Dan performed his exuberant victory skate around the Olympic oval. The roaring cheers of the crowd set the tone of this rare happy ending.

Ethel Sorensen, though ninety-four years of age, was still a lovely woman physically, and mentally she was alert to current news, involved in projects, and insistent that keeping "anxiously engaged" is the key to a joy-filled winding down to a long life. Ethel coined the name "Autumn Eves" for a group she belongs to in her neighborhood. They are older women who have lived full lives. At first they dragged their feet about "going out socially with a bunch of widows." But once they got started, life truly changed for them. They are enthusiastic about planning events for their times together. Evelyn Vernon, by assignment from the bishop to be a special helper and chauffeur for these ladies, spent full time with them for several years. How they loved her! Several times a month she took them out for dinner or to a cultural event. The women learned their way around the community calendar and found there was still a world "out there" that welcomed them! Ethel started recording their events. Soon she dipped into her own past to write her life story, and then with that published, she started work on the life story of her deceased husband. Naturally, Ethel's good example and enthusiasm were contagious. Now daytime activities include helping other "Eves" do the same. Talented Ellen Nielsen Barnes is now recording her fabulous life, including being honored as an American Mother of the Year and her unique years as director of the famed Washington, D.C., "Singing Mothers." Their philosophy is that life isn't over until it is over, and they ensure the happy ending by keeping the now lively.

The setting for another happy ending is Seattle, Washington. It involves youths who take hold of life's challenges in a stunning way and set an example for people of all ages and with diverse problems.

The 1994 youth conference was in the late planning stage when the adult leaders learned that Travis, who suffers from severe cerebral palsy, wanted more than anything to participate in the conference. It seemed an absolutely impossible consideration because the location and activities were strenuous this year. It was to be rough-out camp with a long, arduous hike into the campsite. Tents and sleeping bags were all right for sturdy youth but totally unsuitable for a handicapped person. Besides, adult leaders had heavy responsibilities in such a situation; they couldn't risk having Travis along. But the word about Travis had traveled around among the youth, and two rugged seventeen-year-old young men volunteered to take full care of Travis, if the leaders would just give them the chance. That meant paying their own way but sacrificing their freedom and good time to ensure a safe, happy experience for Travis. It meant carrying him to camp and total care, twenty-four hours a day, once they arrived. They promised to do this and give him the experience of his life. It turned out to be the most important experience of their own lives as well.

After much conversation and careful planning, parental permission and doctor's instructions later, an excited Travis and his two "brothers" made the tedious trek. Of course it was an act of sacrifice and courage, but when they carried Travis into the campground, the brave young man could think of only one thing. He said to his companion, "I've never been to camp before and I've never blown a leader's whistle. Will you let me celebrate being at camp by blowing your whistle?" And he did, with eyes shining. Blowing a whistle was one physical act that Travis could do!

One of the youth who had committed to caring for Travis bore his testimony at the final meeting of the conference. He asked that Travis be wheeled up to the front. Then he paid tribute to him as the most courageous and pleasant camper among them and made a formal presentation to Travis of his "whistle"—much to the incredible joy of Travis. In his tribute, the young man proclaimed Travis to be the sturdiest of spirit, the most courageous example of noble young manhood because of his faith and determination to "do it!" Quoting from Doctrine and Covenants 89:18–21, he said Travis was the prime example in camp of someone who kept the Word of Wisdom and earned the blessing of the fulfillment of the promise that the "destroying angel shall pass by" the obedient as the children of Israel. All agreed, and a suitable ovation thrilled Travis. He might never do it again, but he had done it once with a mighty happy ending.

Elder James M. Paramore offers another perspective about happy endings. "I remember how I felt forty-one years ago when I was taken from a train in Europe at 2:00 A.M. by two soldiers of a hostile nation and held against my will. I was verbally and physically abused. I felt I would never see my family or my country again. I assure you that while I was held captive, the blood coursed through my veins like adrenaline. Though the captivity lasted less than a day, it seemed like an eternity. And when I was put on another train and sent back to safety, my gratitude to the Lord knew no bounds. I was *free!* As I talked to the train conductor, I learned that hundreds had not been so lucky.

"I then was led to think of Him who really delivers us from various types of prisons into forgiveness, a newness of life, of spirit, of change, and of opportunity, and how the souls of men find such relief, fulfillment, and safety when this occurs." (" 'By the Power of His Word Did They Cause Prisons to Tumble,' " *Ensign,* November 1992, p. 9.)

That was a happy ending to a life-threatening experience. Not every one is put to that kind of test. But we all feel pressures and reach for peace and joy under a variety of conditions.

Sunday evening supper is a joyful way for a family to unwind and catch up with each other before the stress of a new week begins on Monday. Such a tradition, well planned, comes within the aura of stopping to smell the flowers on a spring hike. Begin with an attractive table, then a blessing on the food and the mood. As for the supper itself, there are so many easy ways of making food preparation simple that the burden can be light. But the food should be soul-nourishing as well as appetite-satisfying. Spaghetti and meatballs, waffles and strawberry topping, meat loaf and scalloped potatoes, minestrone or clam chowder and baking powder biscuits with frozen raspberry jam, hard eggs in Swiss cheese white sauce, Reuben sandwiches, or grilled bratwurst and sauerkraut. Whatever can be prepared ahead and enjoyed later.

For a glad tiding to share after supper and before the wave of farewell that we talked about in the beginning of this chapter, someone could read aloud: "Now [may] the God of hope fill you with all joy and peace in believing, that ye may abound in hope, through the power of the Holy Ghost" (Romans 15:13). It was on such an occasion that Bill and Marvetta's troubled daughter entered the home just long enough to pick up something she needed to take back to her college dorm. They hadn't seen or heard from her in several months—except the report from a mutual friend that Tammy was into all kinds of serious mischief and had been warned by university officials about being dropped from school. She'd been staying here and there with friends, but now, when she walked in on the Sunday evening setting with all her family about the table enjoying traditional food and quality companionship, her heart turned over in remembrance of such good times with her family. They weren't perfect, and admittedly neither was she, but these were the people who loved her *anyway!* They had similar memories and had bonded because of shared challenges (like the gratitude for heaven's protection during a severe earthquake). They'd experienced the same Thanksgiving dinners at Grandmother's, and oh, those Sunday night suppers!

Enough of these past miserable weeks. She pulled up a chair and sat down to stay when they welcomed her.

People crave happy endings to a book, a movie, a romance, or a sticky, stressful situation. We also yearn for a happy ending to life itself. The story surrounding the passing of Vivian Redd McConkie, mother of Elder Bruce R. McConkie, is a treasure in a collection of happy endings.

She was ninety-five years old and a faithful daily worker in the temple. When the life of her son Bruce was drawing to an end, this remarkably strong woman came to him with a special message reflecting her faith. She said, "Bruce, when you see Daddy, you tell him I'm sitting by the side of the road waiting for him. Tell him to get himself down here and pick me up."

Immediately she began to feel poorly. Three weeks to the day after Bruce was buried, Sister McConkie's body was laid to rest in her grave. In her last moments of life on earth, she suddenly opened her eyes and looked up and beyond family members standing near. With both arms raised and reaching, she exclaimed, "Wow!"

Now, that is a happy ending!

Forever Sunshine

When the Lord is near, then "the dove of peace sings in my heart" and there is sunshine in my soul! What gladness to be rid of the destructive worries of the world—not spared from trouble and stress but peaceful because of living close to the Lord! What hope and happiness that there is no need to fear an enemy or the tempter! No more fretting about seeming personal inadequacy or about being in the midst of strangers or about suffering some strange sickness! It is as the Lord God said to the children of Israel, "When thou goest out to battle against thine enemies, and seest horses, and chariots, and a people more than thou, be not afraid of them: for the Lord thy God is with thee" (Deuteronomy 20:1).

Sunshine. Forever sunshine, no matter what! As long as we behave like children of Israel, followers of Christ.

That is joy.

Heavenly Father will help you make happy endings, help you enjoy exhilarating sunshine in the soul. The Lord doesn't want you held captive from him. You, through your faithfulness, are to succeed and to be happy. It is to be for you as the Psalmist said, "Thou has turned for me my mourning into dancing: thou hast put off my sackcloth, and girded me with gladness." And again, "Weeping may endure for a night, but joy cometh in the morning." (Psalm 30:11, 5.)

And as for me, there is sunshine in my soul because of and in spite of—as the phrase fits—the glad happenings in life. Jesus does show his smiling face, he does raise his healing hand. He is in our midst to ameliorate our suffering, no matter what the details. Faith is the catalyst and experience proves it so.

Now . . . may music begin your day and tranquility sweeten your sleep. And the next time you hear "Happy Days Are Here Again" may you sing along with gusto, knowing it is *your* song, with the encore number being "There Is Sunshine in My Soul Today."

May what Paul wrote to the Romans happen to you—may the God of hope fill you with all joy and peace in believing, that you may abound in hope, through the power of the Holy Ghost (see Romans 15:13). May you be "girded with gladness." May your cup run o'er until forever.

Sunshine. Blessed, forever sunshine!